The

LEGALITEAS *of*
ENTREPRENEURSHIP

To Jeeah,

Yngon This!

Lisa Brown

To Sean,
Enjoy this!
Nathann

The LEGALITEAS *of* ENTREPRENEURSHIP

The Relentless Pursuit
of Excellence and Balance
in Starting Your Own Business

LISA BONNER, ESQ.

BOOKLOGIX·
Alpharetta, GA

The information provided in this book is not a substitute for legal advice, and the author specifically disclaims anything to the contrary. You are advised to consult a licensed attorney in your jurisdiction to give you specific advice tailored directly to your particular legal matter and questions.

ISBN: 978-1-6653-0378-1 - Paperback
eISBN: 978-1-6653-0379-8 - ePub

Library of Congress Control Number: 2022904005

Printed in the United States of America   030822

☉This paper meets the requirements of ANSI/NISO Z39.48-1992 (Permanence of Paper)

*"You have to learn the rules of the game.
And then you have to play better than anyone else."*

— Albert Einstein

TABLE OF CONTENTS

PREFACE

"It is not in the stars to hold our destiny,
but in ourselves."

— Julius Caesar

Over the last few years, people have asked me when I was going to write a book, and my answer has always been the same: "When I have something to write about." I wasn't trying to be flippant, of course, because anybody who knows me knows I always have a lot to say! But having an opinion on various topics and finding a subject you are passionate enough about to spend your time writing a book about are entirely different things. So, I did what I often do: I put a photo of a book on my vision board and left it there for inspiration.

That is how I get inspiration often: I sit with it. Because I know what I know, and I know what I don't know, I knew the idea for my book would come to me. I have a passion for the business of law and entrepreneurs, and I have the knowledge to dispense. In Oprah's words, "This I know for sure." I've owned my successful law firm practice serving entrepreneurs, large and small companies, small businesses in media, tech and business for over 25 years, and heaven knows, people are always looking to "pick my brain" about something entertainment- or entrepreneur-related. But there are enough books out there on how to start your own business or the ABCs of entrepreneurship, so I put a pin in that idea, knowing I needed something to differentiate my book on entrepreneurs from everything else out there.

What I also know is that I am constantly told by others that my life is inspirational, that I have a zest for living. I love my life and I love my job: I am an entrepreneur! Though my life is not perfect, daily I live in joy. I thought at this point I'd have a husband, 2.5 kids and a dog; instead, I have an ex-husband, no kids and two cats! Even though my life didn't exactly turn out as I envisioned, I have made the absolute best out of my life. I have a dope legal practice representing clients in music, television, film and digital industries. I am production counsel for several shows you've probably seen on TV. I represent people who create and write for some of the best shows on television, and you have surely been dancing to some of my clients' music and beats for years. I have my health, an amazing family and some cool ass friends. I am fit, a pretty good cook, and have travelled the world (83 countries at the time of this book's publication). As I hope you can tell, I've managed to balance my professional life with my interests and have a good time while taking care of business in the process.

But I also have my challenges. Life ain't all rainbows and unicorns. Over the past four years, I've lost two parents, one of my closest girlfriends to stage 4 breast cancer, a first cousin who died suddenly and my 16-year-old cat! I went through a midlife "transition," a pre-pandemic breakup and, most recently, a bilateral hip replacement. Yep, your girl needed not one, but two new hips as a result of being rear-ended in an auto accident a few years back. I keep going, I keep working, pursuing excellence, but I do it with grace. I realize that the key to my success has been balance, and I want to share some of this insight with you!

As an entrepreneur, you need the information, and you are definitely going to need balance while pursuing excellence. But starting a business is more than a notion or more than simply declaring yourself an "expert" on social media. Being an entrepreneur isn't for everybody. You have to work like you're working for somebody else, but harder. You need discipline, but to know when to relax. You have to expect the unexpected. You have to be a hustler, but not a con (wo)man. You have to be able to ride the waves of disappointment and successes with equal grace and gratitude. There will be financial ebbs and flows. In other words: must have balance.

Planning is equally important. You must prepare, you must have a vision and a mission in the form of a solid business and contingency plan. No shade, but most people, I've discovered, simply do not plan—and a plan without action is just a wish. Without planning, you are zigzagging your way to success, which in turn affects your mental and financial health. Then you go haywire and get so mired down in the pursuit of establishing a successful business, it's easy to forget that life is passing you by. So, whether you're thinking about starting your business, or you're 10 years in as your own boss and using this book for additional reference, don't forget the pursuit of balance. Being an entrepreneur can easily suck the life out of you, but with proper planning and balance, it can also be one of the most rewarding paths you've ever been on.

I finished most of this book during the Covid pandemic lockdown (after several years of starting and stopping), the economy took a hit, and many lost jobs. The unemployment rate hovered around 15 percent, higher than any time in recent history. For many, setting up shop may be your way to economic stability in these uncertain economic times, and you can bet that Covid gave birth to a lot of small businesses. Even as the pandemic is subsiding and businesses are reopening, retailers and employers can't get people to return to work, as many people have discovered the joy of being their own boss.

So that's what this book is about: how to be prepared to approach your business like a business, but with balance. That is what differentiates this book from other legal texts on start-ups and entrepreneurial endeavors. Sure, I give you the legal insight on how to start a business via a step-by-step analysis. I even give you a few forms to guide you along the way. (Although neither is meant to replace specific legal advice tailored to your needs.)

But I also include practical advice from my first-person perspective that I wish someone had given me prior to beginning my own journey. You know, the kind of advice your granny would have shared with you, had she owned her own salon. Or the advice you and your entrepreneurial girlfriend discovered and are commiserating about over a glass (or three) of wine after graduating from the School of Hard Knocks; the brutal stuff that happens to everyone on the road to success that brings you to your knees, shouting, "Jesus, be a fence!" The stuff nobody tells you about. Yeah, that advice… It's in here! I am spilling all the tea on that practical knowledge in segments I have befittingly titled "Tea Time."

Think of Tea Time not as legal advice, but your practical and real-life GPS that will help you launch a successful business while keeping your sanity. Doing it right from the beginning saves you time, frustration, money and some legal battles easily avoided by proper planning. This book will spill the LegaliTEA on starting your own business and staying sane and balanced in the process!

TEA TIME

It's All About Your Mindset

> *"The best way to predict your future is to create it."*
> — Abraham Lincoln

MINDSET IS so important that I had to kick off the book with this jewel. Because deciding to start your business is one of the most important and professional undertakings you will ponder, you'll need a clear head to sort everything out. Whether you are taking the leap from a nine-to-five and the safety of collecting a check on the first and 15th, or you're starting/restarting your own business, there are many variables to think long and hard about.

When I say mindset is important, I mean a few things. First, this is not the time to wing it, throw caution to the wind, or fly by the seat of your panties. On the contrary, I know Steve Harvey told us to *jump*, but when making that decision, you should have a clear vision of what it is you are trying to establish: What and where are you jumping *to*? What is your brand? How will you position yourself? Your clarity of mind can only be brought about by decluttering your mental and physical environment. A clear mind leads to a clear vision.

I have found meditation to be a great tool. I am not here to sell you on the benefits of meditation; there is undeniable scientific research about this, including reducing stress, and preventing or shortening illnesses. Personally, I have found meditation essential in honing my mental clarity. I try to meditate and have some clarity on a daily basis, even if it's for 10 minutes. You don't need to mediate like a monk trained in transcendental meditation. Just a few deep breaths in a quiet environment and a dedicated time of silent reflection are all you really need. Take time to get centered and connect with the Universe, your Source, your ideas, and let your mind wander. Or just be still and sit in gratitude while listening to calming music or sounds of nature. Think about all the possibilities, your hopes and dreams for your business. See it, taste it, feel it. What would it look like if you *knew* you were destined for success? What would you do with this business if you knew you could not fail? Think about your resources, both current and potential. Think about your client base, your customers, advertising and marketing (both social and traditional media). Let your mind wander; think and dream big! Sit in stillness, write down your thoughts and a plan of action. Repeat, revisit… on a daily basis. That is what I have done over the years. Dream it, plan it, see it, do it!

As for your physical surroundings, some people claim to work "just fine" in clutter. However, there's something to be said for giving things away. You don't need that old Motorola two-way pager, nor do you need to hang onto those old patchwork suede boots you wore in business school. Give it away! If you're in the mindset to be as successful as you know you are going to be, you will be able to afford some new fly boots when the time comes...as you once envisioned in your meditation.

Even if you claim you can work in a messy office (because you "know where everything is!"), throw out some things, free up space and let the law and energy of recirculation into your life! From the practical (i.e., cash) point of view, you'll need the receipts for those donated items later on in the year to offset some of your taxable income with charitable giving. From the spiritual point of view, you need to make space for your vision. You have heard this from everyone when you were talking about that _____ you wanted. You have to clean out your _____ to make room for it in your life. Well, the same goes for your entrepreneurial endeavor. You can't make room for change if everything stays the same. You've got to make space for the new. And that's exactly what you're doing by decluttering your mental and physical space.

Don't worry, this book isn't all New Agey; the next Tea Time won't be on healing crystals, I promise. It will, however, be filled with practical advice. But remember: these are things that have worked for me. And it's undeniable that a clear mind and a clear space clears the path for inspiration to flow. So, let's *go*!!

Chapter 1

MIND YOUR BUSINESS WITH YOUR BUSINESS PLAN

"The beginning is the most important part of the work."

— Plato

WE STARTED this book talking about the importance of having a vision, one that you can taste, see and feel in order to bring your dream to fruition. How you implement this vision is where planning comes in. A well thought out, actionable business plan will give you a clear road map of where you intend to go and how you will get there. *Write it out*! You will need a clear and concise written plan to present to potential investors and others whose interest you are seeking to garner. Whether you are in tech ultimately seeking investment capital or an influencer seeking to work with brands, you will need a clear pitch to your target audience.

The type of plan you'll need will vary greatly depending on your proposed business. If you're seeking investors, they'll want to know how their sought after investment will be spent and how long it will take to make a return. The investor will want to make sure you can clearly demonstrate how much revenue you need, how you'll market your services, and any potential roadblocks or contingencies. Whether you have investors or not, every business plan needs to clearly project and articulate revenue, roadblocks and a sustainable backup.

Look at your business plan as a road map to your success. It should outline your professional background, where you are going and how you're going to get there. This document should also include clear, concise information about your services, what makes you and your company special and how to differentiate yourself from the sea of companies and individuals who invariably offer similar services. Define your needs: What are your start-up costs? Do you require an office or can you work from home? If your answer is office, will a virtual office with conference room and receptionist coverage cut it or do you need a traditional office with four walls and room for staff? Are your products drop shipped or will you need money for a brick-and-mortar store?

Additionally, you need to think about capital: how will you pay yourself and your employees? Many people are shocked to discover the hidden costs of simply running payroll. As an employer, you must pay "Employer Taxes" (social security, Medicare, federal and state unemployment taxes) on each employee's compensation, even when paying yourself. This can potentially double the amount of money you need to simply write yourself and your employees a paycheck. Be clear about start-up costs; once you're in business is no time for surprises. Your plan should have enough financial projections to cover your expenses and carry you through the "ebb" months that may come along. This is your one clear, concise shot to get the interest and investors you need.

Finally, your business plan should contain a marketing overview. Marketing is key to any business and being an entrepreneur is no exception. You have to think of a plan to introduce your goods or services to your target audience and build loyalty in your clients and customers. You cannot rely solely on social media to market your business. Regardless of whether you have 1,000 or 100,000 social media followers, you will still need a marketing plan because social media is a tool—not a platform. In some instances, it's even a popularity contest. You may use social media as a tool to promote your product to followers but it is not a marketing plan, a sales platform, nor a method of distribution. Likes don't necessarily translate into orders or dollars. We all know those people who have large social media followings and have no business; conversely, we have people who own successful businesses who have so few followers, you wonder if they know how to use social media at all (they probably don't; they are out there in real life making it happen). So, let's get to the basics.

A. THE BUSINESS PLAN

1. **Executive Summary:** A clear and concise overview of your company and your company's mission statement; description of your goods and services; your marketing strategy; and what makes your company unique and stand out from the crowd. This section should also include the company's market forecast and projected financials. Here's your one shot to grab people's attention, so make this one-page statement stand out. Consider the Executive Summary the "elevator pitch" of your company and its personnel; these human resources are often key assets in getting your company funded or acquired.

2. **Company Description:** An in-depth description and analysis of your business, its product or service offered, the company structure, employees, officers, and current ownership. Use this section to elaborate on the plans and forecast for the company, necessary infrastructure, and your overall vision, including how its executives and the proposed team can help propel your company to success.

3. **Product or Service Offered:** An in-depth description, including photos of your product or services, and the clear-cut advantage you offer over the competition. Basically,

this section details what you're selling and how you are going to make money. You should also include information on any patents or trademarks for the company and its goods and services. Any protection of your intellectual property is a big plus for investors and distributors because it shows you've already secured the necessary protection to fend off infringers, unfair competition or frauds.

4. **Market Analysis:** This is where you outline your industry, including your involvement in and knowledge of said industry. Anyone pouring money into your business will want to make sure you have a solid understanding of the market and its trends. They want to know that you understand your competition and why your product fills a void in that market. You are the expert and this is the section to let them know it. Show and tell 'em why you are a good investment.

5. **Sales:** An overview of your company's sales history and projection of sales with the proposed distribution and marketing of your product or service.

6. **Investment Sought:** Outline of the financial ask for your company for the near future and how you will utilize this investment to achieve your goal, therefore turning a profit so your investor can realize her return on the investment. You will need funds to create (expand) your website and invest in a CMS (customer management system) to properly market to your clients over email and the internet. Whatever you're offering, you must know how to use this medium to market (or hire someone to do it for you). Outline your growth for your company over the next year, three years and five years out. If you need to reinvest the profit or if you think you will have the need for additional funding, you should also include it here.

If you are an "influencer," your business plan will be focused more so on:

1. **Brand Awareness:** Getting more people to know, recognize and like your brand.
2. **Building Brand Identity:** Engaging people with your brand's personality and core values.
3. **Audience Building:** Growing your audience and garnering more followers.
4. **Engagement:** Engaging your audience,
5. **Generating Leads:** How you plan to garner leads and influencer campaigns.
6. **Sales:** Getting people to buy your services and products. Becoming a brand ambassador.
7. **Brand Loyalty:** Building brand loyalty; how to repeatedly engage followers and customer retention

B. MARKETING PLAN

Depending on the stages of your business, you may need several marketing plans, but the first one you'll need should identify your business' target audience and how to reach them. A winning marketing plan will look something like this:

1. **Overview:** The good news is that you can recycle most of what you created in your business plan's Executive Summary section for the marketing plan's summary. Be sure to make a thorough and powerful presentation for this section. Think of this as your "elevator pitch" to highlight all that is great about your company.
2. **Target Audience:** Identifies your ideal customer, your target demographic and how your product is best positioned to serve them.
3. **Pricing and Positioning:** This section is crucial as this will allow you to identify your potential profit but it also allows you to competitively price your goods and services to

maintain your market share and ward off any competition. There are various pricing models to consider when pricing and positioning your product, and pricing and positioning therefore go hand in hand.

    a. **Premium Pricing:** If you are introducing a new, game-changing product to the market, or if you're offering your customers a competitive advantage, you can set your prices higher and capitalize on this uniqueness of your product.

    b. **Economy Pricing:** If you're entering into a saturated market and want to gain market exposure, lower the prices on your product in an attempt to gain some market exposure and share.

    c. **Price Skimming:** Think of this as halfway point between premium pricing and economy pricing. The gist is simple: prices are set higher upon the initial rollout, maximizing profits then dropping your prices upon market saturation or increased competition.

C. NON-DISCLOSURE AGREEMENTS

Your business and marketing plans are proprietary documents that you will share with others. These plans include valuable company information: the outline of your plans to grow your business, customer lists and trade secrets—all highly confidential information you need to protect. In order to make sure the information and plans you share are kept private, and used as intended, you want to ensure that the people with whom you are sharing are keeping your business confidential. You can do this with an NDA, also known as a non-disclosure or confidentiality agreement, which is an agreement drafted to protect the disclosure's proprietary information against unauthorized use and disclosure by the receiving party.

What exactly is Confidential Information? You need to be clear about what is considered confidential information, because that's what you are trying to protect. A common definition of Confidential Information in an NDA would look something like this: *"Confidential Information" means any oral, written, graphic information including, but not limited to, that which relates to content, programming, research, product plans, client information, products, services, developments, inventions, processes, designs, drawings, engineering, formulae, markets, intellectual property applications, software (including source and object code), hardware configuration, computer programs, algorithms, regulatory information, clinical data and analysis, business plans, agreements with third parties, services, customers, marketing or finances which Confidential Information is designated in writing to be confidential or proprietary, or given orally to the other party regarding the Relationship. For the avoidance of any doubt, all of the foregoing information disclosed regarding the Relationship shall be deemed Confidential Information unless specifically exempt in writing clearly stating otherwise.*

It is important to note that this definition covers all information disclosed and bookended to include virtually all information whether written or oral, and all methods of disclosure unless specifically exempt.

There are a few exceptions to what can be legally protected under the NDA. The exclusions are information that: *(a) was in the public domain at the time it was disclosed or has entered the public domain through no fault of the receiving party; (b) was known to the other party, without restriction, at the time of disclosure, as demonstrated by files in existence at the time of disclosure; (c) is disclosed with the prior written approval of the disclosing party; or (d) is disclosed pursuant to court, administrative or other governmental agency order.*

You want to make sure that your agreement provides a provision regarding keeping your Confidential Information inside the company, so your NDA must include a term, and should also extend to the recipient's employees and people who work with or on behalf of the recipient.

Many NDAs are mutual, meaning both parties agree to keep each other's information confidential. All terms in the agreement pertain equally to both parties, so each party is protected and can openly share ideas with each other on how such a meeting can benefit both parties. If your party is the only party disclosing information, then a unilateral form will suffice. Always try to push for a mutual NDA, as a meeting is an exchange of ideas between two parties. Make sure you get these documents signed and returned to you. Keep copies for your files in the event you need to enforce this. It has been known to happen, and you will have to produce your signed documents.

APPENDIX A: Non-Disclosure Agreement

TEA TIME

Bet on Yourself

"I am not afraid; I was born to do this."

— Joan of Arc

MY FIRST JOB as a licensed attorney was at a mid-sized commercial litigation firm in Los Angeles. I'd moved back to L.A. at the 11th hour after I filed for my divorce in the last semester of law school. Because of this last-minute decision, I'd missed the recruiting season at my law school, New York University, which, because of their rank and stellar reputation (hey, their words, not mine, but no lies told), had a 100 percent graduate placement rate. Meaning, I certainly could have landed the job of my choice at any of the L.A. firms which came to recruit on campus. By this point, I was financially on my own again, so I wasn't particular about the *type* of legal job I was going to take, but I knew that as a recent law grad, I didn't know much about the practice of any type of law, so any firm job was fair game.

Before graduating from NYU, my academic advisor called me into her office and implored me to try and find a job before moving. Surely, some of this was because she cared, but I am just as certain that the entire faculty was giving me the side eye because, yes, your girl was about to throw off NYU Law's 100 percent graduate placement rate. My retort was, "If NYU is half the school it's cracked up to be, I will pass the California bar on the first try and have a job by Christmas!" Let me be clear, I was secure but scared: the California bar has the lowest pass rate in the nation; only about 20 percent of the applicants pass the first time around. But I studied, and was prepared and true to form, I passed the bar on the first try! More on that later. And to top it off, I had a job by Thanksgiving. Money and time indeed well spent!

My first job as an associate was at a commercial litigation firm. One of the named partners, Robert, who happened to be my boss, was a Bankruptcy Trustee, which in layman's speak means that he was tasked with ensuring those who filed for bankruptcy protection (called "debtors") were complying with the rules of the court and the debtors were not engaging in "fraudulent transfers" (giving things away to friends and family, only to get them back after your financial debts are wiped clean; we all know that old trick). I figured that in addition to learning how to litigate (prosecute a case in court), I could also get some experience working with the bankruptcy courts.

What I didn't realize as a young attorney was that the opportunities in entertainment would come to me fast and furiously in L.A., even though entertainment was not my area of expertise. To be young in L.A. means to be out socializing, fraternizing at various conferences and parties; there's always someone who needs an entertainment lawyer. But I was a new commercial litigator, not an entertainment lawyer. I realized that if I didn't pursue learning about entertainment business and entertainment law, I would be missing out on some serious cash and some serious opportunities. But I have always been a studious one and live by the words of Abraham Lincoln: "Give me six hours to chop down a tree, I will spend the first four sharpening the axe!"

My first offer in the industry (shorthand for entertainment industry) was to mark up a management contract. Since I was recently licensed, I was a green lawyer all the way around. So, I figured that while I was learning one segment of the law in the commercial litigation area, I could just as easily learn another sector of the law. I'd just spent three years in law school studying several subjects at once, and another three months studying various subjects for the bar, so the intense preparation this task required was nothing new to me.

I usually arrived at my office by 8:30 a.m. and worked a full day. One of our firm's clients was the Los Angeles Unified School District—the nation's second largest school district. When I started, we were in pre-trial motions and I worked a 12-hour day every day. But once we were finished at work, I would pull out old copies of these venerable law treatises, *Entertainment Industry Contracts*, and read about the topic *du jour*. My boss dabbled in entertainment back in the day, so he let me use the books and would look over my markups on management contracts to ensure I was on track.

But I really struck gold on the bankruptcy side of our practice. When filing for bankruptcy protection, the debtor must turn over, among other things, all executory contracts (documents that are still being fulfilled). One of the debtors under our jurisdiction was a *very* popular, household-name 1990s R&B singer who'd recently filed for bankruptcy citing the oppressive nature of her recording contract which precluded her from making any "real money." The crooner stated that the production company and the subsequent recording company that assumed her contract ate up the bulk of her royalties, leaving her indigent, unable to pay her bills or afford any semblance of a normal lifestyle. Her unfortunate situation was my come up. I had all the copies of her recording agreements: the first agreement with the production company; the second, amended agreement with the production company; and the subsequent agreement she'd signed with the major label. I was able to see the progression in her agreements, how the requirements and the advances, royalties and other payments changed with each contract.

Each night after work-work, you could find me in my office,

burning the midnight oil and pouring over copies of these different agreements with color coordinated pens (those are my jam), notebooks, reference books on the music industry, whiteboards (the real whiteboards with markers—before Smartboards). It was a veritable music industry contracts war room, if you will. Thanks to those documents, books and my sheer willpower, I understood enough to take on my first music client, as long as it didn't interfere with my litigation work.

The moral of the story: If you want something badly enough, you will find a way to make it happen. No one is coming to save you. I wanted to learn the music business, so I did, and I also began to learn and study about the film and television industries. More on that later.

Not long after my marathon study sessions and my first few music agreements, I got a call from one of my bar study partners who'd recently been tapped to flesh out the Business and Legal Affairs department at a streaming startup. Because I'd taken the first few steps toward learning and teaching myself the basics of entertainment law, I had a perfunctory knowledge which perfectly positioned me to step into an entry-level position in the industry.

For this first entertainment job, I took a $30,000 pay cut from my litigator job (which is more like $50,000 in today's money) and was given a three-month "trial period." The new start-up needed to mitigate professional and financial risks. Even though I'd left a prestigious job in litigation and bankruptcy at a successful firm, and had recently been appointed as a Substitute Chapter 7 Trustee (the youngest in California history), I had to prove myself nonetheless. What a coup, huh? Now here I was, delving into unchartered territory. I didn't care. I now wanted to be an entertainment lawyer and as soon as I got that offer, I turned in my written resignation and never looked back. I bet on myself! I knew the odds I'd overcome with the California bar exam, and all the other obstacles I'd stared down in my life, and knew I was prepared to win. Right then and there, I decided I was going to be an asset to the company by making myself in-dispensable, and this three-month gig was going to turn into a full-time offer, which it did.

Not only did it turn into a full-time job, but I also worked there for several years. It was the best of both worlds. A nationwide outside law firm was teaching me the ropes of entertainment law, and I was working in-house at a full-fledged production company, learning all areas of entertainment–not just music, but TV, independent film, touring and merchandising. Through that job, I'd gained legal and personal access to major players which enabled me to negotiate a severance package of roughly $15,000 several years later once the internet bubble began to burst. I took that money, my computer, and my access to clients I'd gathered, many of whom were producers at the company, and launched my own entertainment law firm: Convergence Law Group PC, in Venice Beach, California, with a few other partners from the start-up. We were one of the very few lawyers at the time who had an understanding of e-commerce law and how that fit into music, film and TV. This knowledge worked to our advantage and I haven't worked for anyone since that day. Even when I took a job as Head of Film and TV at Dreier LLP in New York City, I was still my own boss. More piping hot tea on that later! That's a whole lesson. Stay tuned.

You have to have that vision of what you want, and you have to want it badly enough and work like hell to make it happen. Bet on yourself, believe in yourself, and do the work! Let the words of the William Ernest Henley poem "Invictus" guide you: "I am the master of my fate; I am the captain of my soul."

Chapter 2

ESTABLISHING YOUR DREAM TEAM

"To become truly great, one has to stand with people, not above them."

— Montesquieu

HOPEFULLY, by the time you have your business plan ready to go, you'll be looking to establish your dream team. What that looks like depends on what type of business you are going into. But no matter what, we all need good advice to help hone and execute our vision. Products and services don't make the business. People do, that's why they're called "human resources." We can't be the Jack/Jane of all trades in our business; no woman is an island. As the "boss," you may feel like you need to have an intricate understanding of how everything works in your business. That couldn't be further from the truth. Build your team with like-minded people who can help shape, guide and challenge you. You don't need to be the smartest person in the room. In fact, I always say if you're the smartest person in the room, you're in the wrong room!

So, where do you begin when building your dream team? I like to start with culture and mission checks. It's your business, so it's important for you to understand the "culture" you are creating. Think about how you want to serve your clients, what kind of culture you want to create for your employees. At

Convergence Law Group, we were young barristers, and we and our physical offices all had that vibe as the cool-ass lawyers who knew some new sh*t in the internet industry. We knew what others didn't. At Bonner Law, on the other hand, I still know my sh*t, and I have positioned myself as one of the few Black film and TV production lawyers. We deliver "excellence" in a non-intimidating way for the client. I have built my firm of over 20 years with this in mind. Part of my mission statement reads as follows:

"Our mission is simply to provide our clients with state of the art professional and personalized legal services in a manner that is consistent with our beliefs. We believe that the success of our clients is based on a relationship of trust, respect and concern.

"At Bonner Law PC, we take the time to build and to consistently nurture a positive professional and personal client-attorney relationship that facilitates the accomplishment of the clients' legal goals. We believe further that our clients are our business partners and, as such, we strive to create a synergistic, client-friendly, business-like culture and atmosphere that is inclusive and informative."

Everyone I hire has that same level of excellence; likewise, those who I've let go failed to live up to our mission. Define your mission, establish your culture, and hire only those who are consistent with your ethics. You want success *and* you want happy people working with you, because those who enjoy their time at work are likely to be more productive.

Before we get into the dream team, I told y'all I was going to give it to you straight, no chaser, and some real life, practical advice. Since I slid something in about firing people above, here is my take on firing: it sucks, bottom line! But you can't be afraid to pull the plug on someone who doesn't mesh with you, your culture, or who is underperforming. As a business owner, you are going to have to make a lot of tough decisions and keeping someone who isn't working out is one of them, so get used to it. There are ways to protect your company so you (hopefully) won't get sued, provided, of course, there are no extenuating circumstances, such as discrimination or harassment (you cannot legally contract around an illegal behavior).

So, let's get to those essential people on your team that everyone needs, no matter what business you're in: the lawyer and the accountant.

LEGAL

Your lawyer will be your first line of offense *and* defense, so you most certainly want to hire a lawyer very early in your process. Attorneys fall into two distinct categories: transactional and litigation. Transactional attorneys put together contracts; litigators seek to enforce them and can sue on your behalf in the event of a dispute or a breach of contract, whatever type. Rarely are we lawyers both litigation and transactional. When you are beginning your practice, you will need a transactional attorney, but even in the category of transactional attorneys, we are specialists. Just as you wouldn't go to a brain surgeon to treat heart disease, you wouldn't hire an environmental attorney to help with establishing your restaurant business. This may seem obvious, but I have been an attorney over 25 years and I still get calls to help people with *everything*! Very rarely do laypersons know what kind of specialist their "attorney friend" is, and many people incorrectly assume we can handle any and all types of transactions. Newsflash: We can't.

If you are offering stock, you may want to hire a corporate attorney. If you are going to be buying or leasing real estate, there are attorneys who specialize in that. If you are going to sign artists to your newly formed production company, find an entertainment attorney. Whatever your proposed business, you will want to find an attorney who can help you from the bottom up with the *underlying* business related to your company and drafting the contracts that you will need to hire employees, vendors and other independent contractors. But remember, you may—and probably will—need to hire more than one attorney as your business grows.

Alternatively, there may be an instance where you may need to sue someone. Maybe you need to enforce a contract, or sue someone for breach of contract, which is legalese for failing to uphold their end of the contract. You may be sued for a slip and fall on your property. In those instances where you need someone to enforce or defend your company's rights, that is when you may need a litigator. Your transactional attorney may likely only be able to take the case so far, perhaps making calls and trying to settle the case. But when that fails, that's the time you call in the litigation attorney. Many times, my clients have issues with breach of contract, or someone may be infringing on their copyright (more on that later), and they turn to me for help. In those cases, I see what I can do. As their transactional attorney, I'll make some calls on their behalf to get to the root of the issue and try to seek some resolution. If that fails, and we're looking at drawing up a lawsuit, that is outside of my purview, and I'll try to find them a litigator to handle the issue. In many instances, I play the go-between with my client and the litigator, which is called litigation management. I manage the relationship between the litigator and my client (who already has a comfort level with me), and ensure that my client understands the case, and the deadlines and does whatever else is needed for smooth sailing.

When looking for an attorney, ask for referrals from people you trust. Gather questions related to your needs and be prepared to ask the proposed attorney questions about their practice, what types of transactions (or cases, in the instance of litigators) they've handled, how long they've been in practice, how they work, and what their general response time is. Also, you may want to ask about her network. You'll want to make sure she has good working relationships with other attorneys outside of her field of expertise whom she can refer you to when the need arises.

You will also need to know about the firm's billing structure. Can she bill you on a flat rate, retainer or hourly? Money matters matter, and it's always wise to mind your cash flow, but you also have to pay people their worth. In my estimation, it is not only annoying but insulting for someone to try to bargain me down on my prices. Would you walk into a department store and ask them to reduce the price of the shoes you're eyeing because you think they are too expensive? We attorneys are a business, and the fair market value of *my* services may not be the same as another attorney's. I liken my products and services to those you may find in Saks, while others may be Macy's or DSW.

No shade to Macy's or DSW, but I know my worth. Just as those companies have certain factors that affect their pricing and products offered, there are a host of factors that determine an attorney's billing, such as: (1) the benefits resulting from the services rendered; (2) the novelty, difficulty and importance of the issues involved; (3) the skill, experience and prevailing hourly rate of the attorney and the requisite skill level reflected in the representation; (4) the time and labor reasonably required for adequate representation; and (5) the responsibility incurred and fulfilled by counsel. If there is any consolation, attorneys are licensed by our respective state bars, and we take our livelihoods seriously, so most attorneys are going to be honest and reliable and give you what you paid for. If not, there are grievance procedures you can follow, and most retainer letters should set out in plain English how to go about settling your differences with your lawyer. If you don't like their prices, products or services, find another lawyer. There is an attorney out there for you; you may just have to work a little harder to find someone in your price range.

When you do decide on the attorney you are going to work with, make sure you sign an engagement letter. The engagement (or retainer) letter is not a contract between you and the lawyer, as attorney's services are "terminable at will," meaning you can terminate an attorney's services for any reason, with or without cause. Instead, the engagement letter outlines the services performed and the fee structure to which you have agreed. It should also set forth the procedure for what fees are owed upon termination, returning the retainer fee, and dealing with any grievances between you and the attorney. It is important to note that some state bars have minimum economic thresholds before you need to give the client a formal retainer letter. In New York, for example, if the value of services rendered is less than $3,000, the lawyer may waive the formal retainer letter requirement, but no matter what the services, at the very least you should always make sure that you have a written understanding (even by email) of the services and fee structure agreed to by you and the attorney, and an invoice for services.

ACCOUNTANT

Another professional you will need on your team is a reliable accountant, because there are two things that are certain in life: death and taxes. Uncle Sam is coming for his, you can bet on that. The right accountant will save you time and money, providing you various services that are imperative to your company's financial health. An accountant is especially important for entrepreneurs, as it helps the owners, investors and anyone with a financial interest in the business stay on top of the Company's earnings, expenses, profits and losses, which enables the owners to make sound financial business decisions. One of the top reasons small businesses initially fail is due to poor financial management and falling behind in taxes. The poor financial health makes the company "sick" and the interest and penalties on failing to pay taxes will often kill a business. Small business cash flow and other resources are often limited, so accountants are necessary to help the economic health and viability of your business. And we all know that our accountants keep us on track with our taxes and (lawfully) help mitigate any local, state and federal business taxes owed, so think of them as the fiscal physician for your business.

Accountants fall into two categories: traditional accountants and certified public accountants ("CPAs"). Traditional accountants have completed their undergraduate accounting degree, while a CPA has undergone more formalized training, completing 150 hours of coursework on top of the bachelor's degree in accounting, passing the state's CPA exam, and subsequently licensed by the state. Like licensed attorneys, CPAs must take continuing education courses to ensure they stay on top of trends and new rules governing their business and the tax laws. CPAs can perform audits and file documents required by the Securities and Exchange Commission, while traditional accountants are precluded from audits and preparing SEC filings.

OUTSOURCING AND VIRTUAL HELP

You may be wondering why I list outsourcing and virtual assistants as part of your Dream Team. Think about it: As a start up, you are most likely going to have limited resources and an overabundance of things to do. Virtual assistants have been around for quite some time, but Covid clearly underscored that we can actually accomplish tasks and effectively run a company without constant face-to-face interaction. The biggest benefit to your company is reduced labor costs, *meaning* you don't have to pay benefits, which is a major cost saver. Virtual help are independent contractors and they pay for their own expenses and taxes, relieving you, the business owner, of that burden. Additionally, as you need your company to remain scalable, you can hire many of these independent contractors on an as-needed basis. Before you hire even part-time employees, consider outsourcing some of your tasks. Market competition is stiff, and with the uptick in freelancers, rates are more affordable than ever.

Some of the most common virtual help includes:
- Assistant and secretarial work
- Bookkeeping
- Accounting and payroll
- Graphic and web design

- IT and back-end support
- Marketing
- Social media outreach
- Transcription
- Proofreading
- Editing
- Voiceover services

Many websites, such as Fiverr, offer access to a wide variety of independent professionals. The portal allows you to scroll and choose your professional based on their skillset, availability and prices, while offering testimonials based on previous clients' experiences. Upwork, another such site, works the opposite way in that the freelancers are doing the "courting." You place your ad on Upwork's website and various freelance professionals pitch *you* their services. You can peruse the proposals and choose what works for you.

You will have a lot to take on as a start-up, and whatever you can do to streamline your time and your business will help keep you sane and in balance. Remember, no woman is an island, and we all need help sometimes. I can't think of anything better than getting help and saving money at the same time!

TEA
TIME

Be Careful Who You Get into Bed With

*"It is difficult but not impossible to conduct
strictly honest business."*

— Mahatma Gandhi

BEFORE DECIDING which corporate structure you should form,
you need to decide whether or not you are going to go at it solo
or have "partners" in your new business. If you are choosing to
partner, keep in mind the old adage: Be careful who you get into
bed with. The quote resonates because it's true in life and in
business.

Here is some piping hot TEA for you; a cautionary tale, if you
will. In 2008, I left L.A. to work with a law firm whose managing
partner, Marc Dreier, was sentenced to prison while I was working as a partner at his law firm. His crime was so notorious,
CNBC chronicled Marc in one of their episodes of *American
Greed*. Here's how it started.

In 2007, after 10 years of practicing L.A., and six of those as
my own boss, a New York power lawyer, Marc Dreier, began to
really pursue me heavily to become a member of his then-
expanding firm. Having recently expanded his firm by opening
a Santa Monica office, Marc was ostensibly planning world law
firm domination by luring away some of the best and brightest

legal minds from traditional firms by treating lawyers as persons and not like chattel, paying the lawyers fairly. He dangled the solo practitioners the security of a steady income and first-class benefits (versus the tradition law firm method of lawyers taking draws and paying them back a percentage of their income). Marc was on a mission, and he was successful. His law firm had moved to the West Coast, and he was adding to his entertainment practice and celebrity attorney roster.

By now, Marc employed 350 attorneys, a few hundred staff members and had offices in four states. Marc was the sole partner in Dreier LLP, a limited liability partnership. After a few meetings, Marc offered me a job as the head of Dreier's Motion Picture and Television practice. But after 10 years in La-La Land, I wanted to go back to New York, and after some fancy negotiations on my part, he agreed. I packed up my life and my law firm in L.A., moved my clients and my practice back to New York City and began working in my plush corner Park Avenue office in Dreier's headquarters on the Upper East Side, where the firm and its lawyers ran like a well-oiled machine.

Until one day, almost a year to the day after I arrived, everything changed.

One gloomy Wednesday in December, the partners were called into the firm's large conference room unexpectedly; this had never happened. We sat there, wondering what was going on; an impromptu partner meeting in the middle of the day must be important, I remember thinking, as this gathering was costing the firm a ton of money in billable hours. We sat in silence until one of the firm's lawyers who'd been with Marc since the beginning came in to tell us that Marc had been arrested! Say what now? I sat there, incredulously trying to process this. Yep, arrested! Turns out, Marc was detained in Toronto earlier in the day for running a Ponzi scheme by impersonating a Canadian pension attorney. Over the previous four years, Marc's Ponzi scheme bilked 13 different hedge funds out of nearly $400 million dollars! To make matters worse, some of that money was used to pay our salaries, and fund and furnish the firm. Marc used the rest of that money to originate and sustain his very lavish lifestyle: he owned a $10.4 million penthouse in New York's Columbus Circle, replete with original artwork, and a huge house in the Hamptons, where he eventually bought the house next door so he could be, in Marc's words, his "own next-door neighbor." Marc's crime was so atrocious, it quickly landed him 20 years in federal prison. *Vanity Fair* magazine eventually dedicated an entire case study on Marc's criminal mind and you can still find his episode of *American Greed* on demand and reruns.

Because Marc committed those crimes on his own accord, unbeknownst to any other attorneys or staff in the firm and used some of that embezzled money to pay us our salaries, the partners wondered where that left lawyers and staff who worked with him, even though none of us had any inclination of his crimes, much less were involved in his horrendous house of cards. Could we be implicated or indicted because of our employment association with him and Drier LLP? Would we be held liable for the firm's debt? Could the Bankruptcy Court hold me liable and put me on the hook for the millions of dollars Marc swindled?

And herein lies the lesson of the importance of choosing your corporate structure and affiliation wisely, which we delve into in the next chapter.

Dreier LLP was an entity owned solely by Marc Drier. Although I was a "partner," I was not a "Partner" in the legal sense and I was not *in* partnership with or an equity partner in Dreier LLP, rather I was an *employee* of Dreier LLP with a Partner title. I'd wisely insisted on an employment agreement prior to my starting at Dreier that specifically stated that I was an employee, not a partner with Dreier LLP or a partner of Marc Dreier, therefore I had no responsibility for Marc's actions which may have impacted the firm, nor did nor I share in any of the financial debts and criminal liabilities facing the firm through his company.

The firm was ultimately dissolved by the Bankruptcy Court and a Bankruptcy Trustee (my former gig) began to examine all of the firm's contracts and bills. Because I had an executed employment agreement, and clearly had no nexus to the situation, I was never brought in for questioning nor under any suspicion at the firm. However, if Marc and I had a different business entity, such as a general or equity partnership, or if I was a part of Marc's company or corporate structure, or even if I had not fully executed any paperwork, the situation could have been much more difficult for me to unravel from, despite the fact that I was utterly and completely blameless. I'll explain more in depth in the next chapter about how all of this comes together. Just know that "guilty by association" holds true in many corporations, LLCs and partnerships.

So, when the firm imploded, I rolled my clients right out with me—literally. I packed up my books, client files and folders and rolled them out with a hand truck to a Town Car waiting outside at 499 Park Avenue. I worked from home until I found another office a few weeks later, and re-formed my professional corporation, Bonner Law, PC without missing a single beat or losing a single client.

But I wasn't off scot-free. Marc nor Dreier LLP offered corporate or company cards, so I charged all my business expenses on my personal American Express and was supposed to be reimbursed. I was reimbursed over the year for some expenses, but on that fateful December day of Dreier's demise, I had approximately $25,000 in expenses outstanding on my *personal* card. I was liable to American Express for those debts and had to pony up that money. In some instances, you can charge off bad debts against your taxes, but that doesn't mean that you can get out of paying your creditors. Another reason it pays to have a CPA on your Dream Team to help you navigate those waters.

Let this be a lesson. I can't reiterate enough, aside from the obvious advice of keeping your hands clean: Choose how you engage with people and who you engage with wisely. And if you do go into business with someone, do so fully knowing what that means for you financially and legally. Pick your association wisely and keep copies of your signed agreements so that you can produce them readily. In my instance, I was not legally Marc's partner, nor did I have any business structure that could have rendered me guilty by association. Rather, I was an employee so I was not held accountable legally and financially — for his crimes, or those committed in the firm's name, but I did have to pay off my unreimbursed credit card expense, as that debt was between me and American Express.

If we had a partnership, LLC or corporation together, I could have had certain accountabilities to his victims and creditors, have potentially lost my license, and owed millions of dollars, irrespective of any wrongdoing on my part. The right corporate structure, employment paperwork and proper paperwork and management can protect you! Insist on it.

Chapter 3

CHOOSING YOUR
BUSINESS STRUCTURE

*"If the first button of one's coat is wrongly buttoned,
all the rest will be crooked."*

— Giordano Bruno

OVER TEA, we just discussed my dodging a bullet because I was not in partnership nor in a corporate or other entity that could have caused me to be liable personally and professionally for Marc's actions or Dreier LLP. That is precisely why your business entity matters. Forming certain entities makes you responsible for the debts and liabilities of the company and in some instances, the malfeasance of your business partners. Therefore, whether you are a one-man band, or if you are thinking about going into business with another person(s), you need to be clear about what potential financial and legal responsibilities each business structure brings into play.

Ponder these questions. I mean, really think this out: Will you need a partner? What do the other person(s) bring to the table? Be mindful that not everyone shares your work ethic, dedication and honesty. By going into business with people, remember that you are potentially responsible for their debts, liabilities and wrongdoings. Although intending to shield the member of the

LLC or corporation from personal liability you are not totally insulated vis-à-vis the corporate structure. Most people will tell you that having a partner is difficult (*raises hand*); more often than not, one person is pulling more weight than the other. Friends often turn into foes over money, so decide carefully whether or not you should have business partners. You can do all of the due diligence in the world, and dot all of your I's and cross your T's. However, in spite of all that, you will invariably have run-ins with a shady partner or company. From fraud, misappropriation of money or trade secrets, it happens to the best of us. Forewarned is forearmed.

Your business entity is the root from which everything else will grow, but you have time to think of what form your structure will take. Be advised that you don't have to decide on your structure immediately or even when you're testing out your products and services to see what is going to stick. What you are selling and how you are selling may eliminate or require a certain entity formation. But you should be ready to choose your business structure by the time you are ready to introduce your service or products into the stream of commerce (aka conducting formal business, with an exchange of money).

Different structures require different formation formalities and filings, and present different tax issues and consequences. A partnership doesn't legally require any formation by way of written documents; if you are in business with another person, by default you have formed a partnership (but the partners should at least draft a simple agreement that sets forth the terms of the partnership—more on all of this below). Exactly what entity you should form is a more involved matter, because each business structure has a unique set of restrictions and formalities.

Let's look at the different entities and what each requires.

A. SOLE PROPRIETOR AND GENERAL PARTNERSHIPS

If you choose to start your business on your own, without forming any corporate entity, you will be doing business as a

Sole Proprietor. Similarly, if you are going into business with some other person(s) and you forgo establishing a formal business entity, you will, legally and by default, have formed a General Partnership. Only if the sole proprietor or general partners want to use an assumed name for the business are you required to file any paperwork, such as a Fictitious Name Statement or DBA (Doing Business As) application with your Secretary of State's office. Because you don't have any state or federal filing requirements or filing fees, these structures are easy; so, *poof*, you're "in business." But there are downsides.

The most notable drawback is that you have unlimited personal liability of the partnership's (i.e., business') debts and liabilities, including any tortious acts committed by you or your partners individually during the course of your business. (Remember my near miss with Marc Dreier?) Further, you won't be able to lure investors with a partnership (see chapter 4) as investors do not, as a rule, want to be subjected to the personal liabilities of your business.

Even though there are no filing requirements to establish a General Partnership, at the very least you should enter into a Partnership Agreement with your business partner to set out the formalities of the business. Ideally, the partnership agreement should cover the term (length of time you are proposing to be in business), the revenue split between the parties, each person's ownership percentage, who is going to manage the business, ownership of the assets, terms to admit other partners, how to dissolve the partnership, and what happens upon death or dissolution. This is especially important because otherwise, each person is, for the most part, personally responsible for the debts, liabilities and taxes of the business in equal proportion, irrespective of their contributions.

Neither a sole proprietorship nor a partnership give you any type of tax benefit or tax break. Although the partnership itself is not taxed on the income from the business, each of the partners is taxed on his or her share of the income from the partnership. All of the income from the business is passed through to the individual tax returns of the owner. In the instance of partnerships, for IRS purposes, each partner is equally responsible for the debts and tax liabilities of the business. Choosing to formally establish your business entity, on the other hand, allows you to adjust the liabilities of the individuals according to their governing documents or any other way the owners choose.

B. LLC vs. CORPORATIONS

If you are serious about your business and you are about to enter your goods or services "in the stream of commerce," then you should consider formalizing your business structure. The purpose is twofold: First, when properly utilized, choosing a formalized business structure such as an LLC or corporation is designed to shield the individual from the debts and liabilities of the business, which, when properly registered and run, those debt and liabilities are limited to the assets within the company. Secondly, it's meant to be a tax vehicle, and when the S Corporate election is chosen, you escape double taxation, paying taxes on income at the business and personal levels.

Now that we've answered the *when* and *why*, let's discuss the *where*. Meaning, in what state should you register your company? It's important to note you can register in any state, regardless of whether you live there and regardless of whether you plan to operate your business there. Some may want to file in a different state because in the instances of Florida or Nevada, there are no personal or state income taxes, or Franchise Tax fees that otherwise exist in Texas and California. Although it seems tempting, there is a caveat: if you do not live in the same state where you register your company, you must register your company as a "foreign entity" to qualify to do business in that state. You will, in all likelihood, have some reporting and filing requirements and fees in the state where you live and/or are doing business.

Let's say you live in New York. You've registered your company in Florida, but as a resident of New York you now have to register your company in New York state as a "Foreign Entity," and you also have to pay taxes on the income that you bring home. As you will learn later in this chapter, LLCs and S Corporations are designed to avoid "double taxation" (paying taxes at the corporate level, then again at the personal level). So now you are paying taxes twice and two sets of filing fees and reporting, and more often than not, all of this hassle for the start-up entrepreneur just isn't worth it.

Many people want to register in Delaware because they've seen so many other people do that. If you ask why they registered the LLC in Delaware, they probably wouldn't know the answer. The truth is, many states have leveled the playing field for the average business and entrepreneurs, and most states afford the companies the same or similar benefits as registering in Delaware. Many larger corporations (C Corporations) are registered in Delaware. As of 2014, more than 64% of Fortune 500 companies were registered in that tiny state, which has less than a million residents. Delaware has very corporate-friendly laws, tremendous flexibility in corporate organization and management, and doesn't require the disclosure of corporate officers or directors. Delaware also has tax benefits: Taxable corporate income earned in other states are exempt in Delaware, but it doesn't work the other way around; if you are not a Delaware resident, you'll still have to pay taxes from income earned in Delaware in your home state. Delaware has a dedicated Court of Chancery, which focuses solely on corporate law and disputes. So, if your company is incorporated in Delaware and that company is sued, you have a dedicated court that has precedential case law and your case is heard and decided by a judge (not a jury) that is familiar with corporate law.

In the instance of most entrepreneurs and start-up scenarios, these reasons don't make it worth the extra hassle of incorporating in Delaware. Additionally, if you register your company in Delaware, you need to have a Delaware registered agent. If you don't know someone personally, you'll have to pay a fee to hire a registered agent. And Delaware imposes a franchise tax that is based on the par amount of your shares issued, and if the corporation is sued, you may have to travel to Delaware to defend the case. Technology companies and larger businesses, however, still may prefer the corporate-friendly laws and flexibility afforded to companies in Delaware and choose to register as a C corporation in the state. But for other business endeavors, it's not worth the extra step.

If you are going to formalize your business, chances are you will form a limited liability company or a Corporation. While both the LLC and Corporations limit your liability and offer tax benefits for the owners, there are some fundamental differences in ownership, filing requirements, stock ownership and transferability, and self-employment taxes that can tip your decision one way or the other.

Let's start with the similarities. Both the LLC and Corporations, when properly filed and maintained, shield the owner from debts and liability incurred from the business. Meaning if the business is sued, only the assets of the entity are at risk, not your personal assets. Both the LLC and S Corporations offer "pass through taxation," meaning business income isn't taxed at the corporate level; instead, profits and losses flow from the business to the owners' personal taxes.

The biggest differences between the LLC and Corporations are taxation, restrictions on ownership, and equity participation. Corporations have the most filing and maintenance restrictions, while LLCs have the least. The table on the next page briefly outlines the differences:

	LLC	S Corporation	C Corporation
Formation	• State registration	• State registration • IRS Form 2553	• State registration • (Default corporate type)
Taxation	• Pass-through taxation • May elect an S Corporation status with IRS	• Pass-through taxation • Income of corporation is taxed at the owner's level of taxation **after the election of S Corporation status** with the IRS	• Pay taxes on corporate income and personal income tax on dividends paid • Default taxation model for corporation
Ownership	• Owned by Members • Unlimited members • Open to Non-U.S. citizens as owners • May be owned by another LLC	• Owned by shareholders • Limited to no more than 100 shareholders • Owners must be U.S. citizens or permanent U.S. residents • May not be owned by another corporate entity or type	• Owned by shareholders • Unlimited number of shareholders • Open to foreign investors • May be owned by another corporate entity
Stock	• N/A • LLCs may issue membership certificates	• Limited to one class of stock	• May offer multiple classes of stock

C. FORMING A LIMITED LIABILITY COMPANY

An LLC is a legal entity, created under state law, but an LLC is not a "corporate" business structure. (Though often erroneously used interchangeably, LLCs are not *corporate* entities.) The LLC may have one or several members and is used to hold assets, such as real estate, or an LLC may be formed to run a business. In order to gain maximum asset protection and tax liability, it must be set up and run correctly, and I'll walk you through those steps here. Although it's relatively easy to establish, let's get into the specifics of how to ensure it's handled appropriately:

1. **Formation**: LLCs exist under state law and are created by the Secretary of State's office. It's a fairly straightforward process; you fill out the statement of formation, which requires some personal information of the proposed owners, and you need to select officers for the LLC (president, vice president, treasurer, secretary), and define what the members' ownership percentages will be. If your LLC transacts business in a state other than the one in which it is organized, as discussed earlier, you will need to register your LLC in the other state.

   Some states have additional steps in order to complete the registration. New York state, for example, has a name publication requirement. Before completing your LLC formation, the LLC must publish the name of the LLC in local newspapers for objection. California, Texas and Delaware require you to pay a Franchise Tax. Check with your particular state to make sure that no additional steps are necessary to complete the registration process, because failing to complete these steps means that your LLC is not properly filed and licensed to do business.

   You must keep your LLC's information current with the state. This is called being in "Good Standing." Don't get alarmed, it's pretty simple. In order to do this, most states require filing annual reports or statements of information and paying any fees owed to the state in which the LLC is organized. The states generally send out a registration form to the email or address on file, but it is incumbent on the LLC managers to keep the registration current. If you fail to timely file or update the required information, the LLC risks dissolution or suspension. Many companies check the state's database to ensure that the company they are intending to do business with is in "Good Standing." If you haven't kept abreast of the annual registrations, you may not be able to collect income until this issue is resolved and the LLC is reinstated.

2. **Operating Agreements**: Once you form the LLC, you must formalize and sign the Operating Agreement. This is the fundamental document that will govern the purpose, management, decision making, capital contribution, and profits and losses of the company. It also sets forth the provisions for transferring and adding members and what happens upon death of the members or dissolution of the LLC. It is all contained in this document. Let's take a look at these individually:

   Purpose: Although the LLC formation generally allows for said LLC to be formed for "any lawful purpose," your Operating Agreement should specifically state the name, the purpose for which it was formed, and the state having jurisdiction over the LLC. This section will also set forth the address of the company, as well as the registered agent's address to formally receive legal and other notices on behalf of the company.

   Term: Some states require a finite term while others allow for an open-ended term; that is, it operates until the LLC is formally dissolved by the parties pursuant to the Operating Agreements. (Don't forget to dissolve the LLC formally with the state or you may run afoul of taxes and other mandated filing requirements.)

   Management: Some LLCs are "Member Managed," meaning they are run by a majority vote of the members of the LLC. Other LLCs are "Manager Managed," where a formal management team is responsible for the overall running of the company as well as its day-to-day activities. There are important and crucial distinctions that should be addressed. In the instance of Manager Managed, although the members still own the LLC, their interests are more passive in that they don't actually manage the business. The members do have some say in the management of the LLC, since they elect the managers and must approve major decisions (i.e., sale of the assets of the LLC; other powers are outlined in the operating agreement). But the LLC may only act through its managers, not the members as a whole.

There are other distinct differences as well. In Member Managed LLCs, the members work together to manage the LLC and each has a vote in business decisions. Binding agreements or contracts must be approved by a majority, and no member is permitted to unilaterally act on behalf of the company. Actions by the members are taken at meetings or by written consents signed by all members, through the adoption of formal resolutions.

Managers, on the other hand, do not need to act as a group in all situations. Each manager has the authority to bind the LLC by his or her own action. But if there are disagreements among managers about particular actions or about management policy, these disagreements should be resolved by a vote.

Members and Membership Provisions: LLC members and their titles, if any, are listed on the initial formation documents, along with the members' ownership percentages, which is often but not always based on their capital contribution. Membership provisions should also set forth how new members are permitted to join the LLC and transfer ownership. It is common to allow new members to transfer ownership only by a majority vote of the existing members. It is important to clearly set forth this provision to avoid any unnecessary discourse between the members after your business is up and running. You should also clearly state that the members will not be liable for the debts and liabilities of the LLC in the due course of business.

Just as the Membership provisions outline what members can do, it is equally as important to state what the members are not allowed to do with respect to the money and property of the LLC. Remember, the LLC is a separate entity and transactions must be treated as such, not as a member's personal property. Common restrictions include the prohibitions that no single member, without proper approval, may:

- Enter into any contract on behalf or for the benefit of the LLC
- Assign, convey, sell, transfer, pledge or encumber any contracts, property or intellectual property of the LLC
- Accumulate debt or make a promise to pay creditors
- Approve or enter into a judgment on behalf of the LLC
- Borrow money in the name of the LLC

Capital Contributions: How much each member is contributing to the LLC is outlined here. Capital contributions are generally proportional to the amount of equity ownership ultimately given to the member. It is customarily not required that members be obligated to contribute additional capital, so, if no contributions are being made, make this clear as well. If members contribute additional capital, the operating agreement should set forth how that contribution will be accounted for and repaid, either through granting additional equity or increased disbursement.

Allocation of Profits and Losses: This section sets forth how net profits are calculated, when the profits will be distributed and what happens in the event of losses. Also, how the profits and losses are allocated amongst the members, and how each is defined.

Accounting: In order to file your taxes properly, you will need to decide when your company's taxable year will end. If your company is using a fiscal year, that means your company will use a different tax year than the calendar year, which needs to be noted for tax preparation. The members also need to decide on whether a cash or accrual method will be used; the method will dictate when and how income is earned and reported for tax purposes. The LLC must also decide if it is going to be taxed as a partnership or a corporation by filing the S Corporation election, as all members of the LLC are taxed the same.

Dissolution: Some states have a finite term for the LLC. Most states have allowed for an open-ended term, which allows for the dissolution of the LLC by agreement of the members, death, or operation of law (i.e., bankruptcy). Upon the dissolution, the affairs of the LLC should be wound up and any remaining capital be distributed as otherwise outlined in the operating agreement.

3. **Must Be a Separate Entity:** In order to obtain limited liability for members, it is critical that your LLC is operated as a business entity that is separate from its members. You may not use the LLC for personal affairs, and money may not be commingled with personal money either. If the LLC is not operated as a separate entity, the existence of the LLC may be ignored, and you may lose the liability protection afforded to you personally.

> **Adequate Assets**: In order to function as a separate entity, your LLC needs sufficient assets to operate its business. At the time the LLC is formed and you execute your Operating Agreement, you will need to contribute sufficient cash and other assets to the LLC to provide it with a reasonable chance of being successful. You should not, for example, loan to your LLC a majority of the funds or assets that are needed to operate the LLC's business. Rather, the funds or assets required for LLC operations should be contributed to the start-up capital of the LLC and noted in the capital contribution section.

Similarly, you should not plan to make substantial distributions of assets until the LLC has earned profits from which to make the distributions. No distributions may be made to members in any case if the effect of those distributions would be to render the LLC insolvent or prevent it from paying its obligations as they become due in the ordinary course of business.

Separate Assets: As a separate entity, your LLC needs to have its own assets. The LLC must maintain its own bank accounts and should hold title to its assets in its own name. Under no circumstances should personal funds, assets, or accounts be mixed with LLC funds, assets, or accounts. LLC funds should never be used to pay personal expenses of members, to make personal investments for members, or for any other purposes not related to the LLC's business. The LLC should not transfer any of its cash or other assets to its members except as reasonable compensation for services by members that have been agreed upon in advance, for reimbursement of members for reasonable expenses incurred on behalf of the LLC, and distributions allowed under the terms of the operating agreement. The LLC's operating agreement may, for example, require distributions to members to enable them to pay income taxes on the LLC's income and may permit other distributions with the approval of the managers.

If the LLC is to use assets owned by a member, appropriate arrangements should be made and documented. For example, a member can lease an office or piece of equipment to the LLC, but there should be a written lease agreement, and the terms should be fair to the LLC; don't go leasing a simple laptop computer to your business for $5,000 a month! If it seems shady, it probably is. The idea is always to stay above the fray.

Separate Operations: The LLC should be operated as an entity separate from its members. All business of the LLC should be conducted in the name of the LLC, and the LLC's name should be used on all agreements, contracts, leases, orders, and other arrangements entered into by the LLC. This company name should also be used on all products, signs, advertisements, correspondence, business cards, directory listings, and similar items. The LLC will need to obtain and carry its own insurance and to file its own returns.

4. **Taxation**: An LLC for federal tax purposes, whether owned by multiple owners or single owners, is by default a "disregarded entity." As the name implies, the business itself is technically *disregarded* (overlooked) for *income* tax purposes and the business income is "passed through" to the members' personal taxes by way of the appropriate IRS 1040 forms, and income is taxed at the personal level.

   When paying yourself income from the LLC as a "disregarded entity," you are paying yourself a "reasonable value of your services"—not a salary. As you are not paying yourself a salary, as a disregarded entity member, you do not pay Federal, State or Local income taxes at the business level. Instead, you file all income earned and paid to yourself through the LLC (for your "reasonable value of services") under your personal income tax's Schedule C on your Federal Form 1040, and pay your taxes based on taxes on that income you paid to yourself. Remember, since you are not an "employee" of the LLC, the LLC member doesn't pay self-employment taxes (Social Security taxes and Medicare). Instead, the LLC pays any self-employment taxes on the business profits when it files the LLC taxes. The catch here is, you are still paying these self-employment taxes on profits, and since you and the LLC are one and the same, you, the member, will be taxed on all business profits.

   There have been many legal changes and challenges regarding paying independent contractors who own an LLC but elect to stay as a disregarded entity. Technically, because the income is passing through to the member(s') personal income tax, the independent contractor is supposed to use her personal social security number on the W9, and not the LLCs EIN. This often presents a problem for the vendor as the vendor needs to properly invoice the LLC.

LLC members may elect to change this "pass through" default taxation by choosing S Corporation status by filing IRS Form 2553 (Election by a Small Business Corporation) within 75 days after the date of the LLC formation. By electing S Corporation status, you may lower your tax burden primarily by changing the way profits are taxed. With the S Corporation election, you are now considered an employee in terms of tax treatment; you pay yourself a salary versus "reasonable compensation" for your services. The LLC member(s) pay into income taxes at the Federal, State, Local level by way of payroll deductions, and pays the self-employment taxes (Medicare and Social Security) through payroll deductions. Any *profits* paid as *distributions* are not considered wages paid to LLC members with the S Corporation election, and therefore are not subject to self-employment taxes (Social Security and Medicare), so this S Corporation election affords the LLC member to lower their personal tax burden.

To ensure compliance, as a professional recommendation, I suggest using a payroll company or signing up with your bank's payroll service to ensure you are properly filing and paying taxes. You will be busy enough handling all of the other aspects of your business, and the small fees that payroll services charge are worth it to ensure all your local, state and federal taxes are filed appropriately and paid timely.

If your LLC fails to file the S Corporation election timely, either because you simply forgot or didn't realize that this tax structure would benefit your company, you may still seek to avail the LLC of the S Corporation election. Existing

LLCs must first file Form 8832 (Entity Classification Election), and then submit Form 2253, with an explanation of your "reasonable cause" for late filing. There is no "magic language" that the IRS is looking for in order to grant the election; there is no published list of reasons. But history has demonstrated the IRS is fairly lenient when granting the late election. The IRS is always looking for accountability of any potential money otherwise owed to the government, so it is important to address how the LLC's financial and tax affairs were handled during the time elapsed between formation and time when the LLC is seeking the election, as the S Corporation election is granted on a prospective, going-forward basis. If you file for the election midyear, and the S Corporation is granted, you will be responsible for filing returns based on both entities.

D. ORGANIZING A CORPORATION

Corporations are the most complicated of all the business entities and the most regulated. However, corporations also offer the greatest liability protection for owners and shareholders. They also have the most ongoing formalities, so let's make sure we organize this appropriately.

1. **Formation**: Like LLCs, corporations are formed at the state level, and are subject to state filing and maintenance requirements. In order to maintain compliance, all required fees should be paid and formalities adhered to as required, or you risk having your corporation suspended.

   In some states, "professionals" (the states' words, not mine) are not allowed to form an LLC. Instead, their professional services must be rendered through a "Professional Corporation." For example, in California and New York, attorneys, dentists, physicians, chiropractors, architects and other "professionals" must form a professional corporation (a "PC"), and are not permitted to have LLCs or any other structures, so that decision is automatically made for you.

2. **By-Laws**: A corporation's formal governing documents are known as By-Laws (as opposed to the Operating Agreements used with LLCs). The by-laws are drafted by the initial shareholders and address the corporation's primary purpose. Much like the operating agreement, the By-Laws outline the procedural operations of the corporation; mandate corporate governance by the officers and directors; and establish procedures for shareholder meetings. By-Laws also address stock issuance, sale, amendments, and admission of new shareholders.

3. **Taxation**: The default tax status for the corporate structure is a C Corporation structure, which causes double taxation because the corporation is taxed separately from its owner. The corporation pays taxes on dividends paid to the shareholders (you, the owner) at the corporate level; you as the shareholder then pay personal income tax on money distributed and paid to you as income or salaries.

    As an entrepreneur, you want to legally keep as much money in your company (and pocket) as you can and not overpay in taxes. By choosing the S Corporation (S Corp) election, you are availing yourself of the "pass through" taxation benefit where the business' profits and losses are instead "passed-through" from the business and reported on the owners' personal tax returns, foregoing double taxation. Any tax due is paid at the individual level by the owner's Federal 1120 forms.

    Most entrepreneurs will probably elect S Corporation status which provides for the taxation of corporate monies only when dispensed to shareholders. Most entrepreneurs, for obvious reasons, prefer the S Corporation election. The S Corporate structure has many more restrictions than the C corporation, including limitations on ownership; therefore, all shareholders of the corporation must agree to choose to elect S Corporation status. These same restrictions are why larger, publicly held corporations are C Corporations. Remember: The S Corporation election must be filed with the IRS within 75 days after formation, but the same exceptions for late filings hold true for a corporation as they do for an LLC. You may file late, provided you have reasonable cause, but this in no way guarantees you will be granted the election.

4. **Separate Entity**: Like an LLC, the corporate entity is separate and legal; therefore, like a person, the corporation may enter into contracts, lend and borrow money, sue and be sued—but in order to maintain its "separateness," the corporation must have adequate and separate assets from that of its shareholders and owners. The corporation must also maintain completely separate operations: All business should be entered into under the name of the corporation and be paid for out of the corporation's accounts and should have separate insurance and file its own taxes—all separate and apart from its shareholders and owners.

Regardless of whether you choose an LLC or a corporation, there are a few additional steps that people, especially those who don't use an attorney or a CPA, seem to forget.

In order to open a bank account or to invoice anyone, if you are formed as a corporation, you must obtain an employer identification number (EIN), otherwise known as a tax ID, from the IRS, which you may liken to your company's social security number. This is a unique number assigned to the entity by the IRS for income and tax purposes. You may apply online or by phone (be forewarned that hold times seem to go on infinitely) and submit Form SS-4. When you begin to invoice for your goods and services, most vendors will ask for the company's EIN before your invoices may be paid. If you are an LLC, you can technically use your social security when filling out a W9, but many LLCs do not want their owner's social security number floating around, and elect to obtain an EIN instead, but that may be an issue with the vendor.

Several states, like Texas and California, require you to pay a franchise tax within a certain number of days after formation. Failure to register and pay the tax may render your company's formation null and void, or you may be suspended from doing business in that state until that is rectified. This is a tax levied by the states for the privilege of doing business in that state. Essentially, another revenue vehicle for the state.

Most states require you to register for permits and licenses with the appropriate agency. If you are selling goods, you will most likely need to obtain a retail license; if you are selling liquor, you must apply for a liquor license; if you are selling services, such as cosmetology, you will be required to obtain a specific license. Never to be one-upped by the federal government, states have their own taxing agencies, so you will have to apply for a state withholding identification number in addition to the EIN. Trickling all the way down, counties, towns and municipalities often have their own local licensing and tax departments, so don't forget to check in with the requirements for each of those. We're dispensing all the LegaliTEA you need to operate like the savvy entrepreneur you are, so be warned that late notices and delinquent fees on your corporate formation add up, which cuts into your business and ultimately your personal and business cashflow. Ultimately, the hassles of formation are worth the benefits, so when you're ready to put those goods and services into the stream of commerce, now you'll know what to do.

TEA TIME

Flexibility Is Key

"Life is a balance on holding on and letting go."

— Rumi

LISTEN, this is the cold, hard truth: we all think we have the best idea west of the Mississippi and our product is going to set the world on end. I get that, because if we didn't think it was a good idea, we wouldn't have come this far. But just because we think it is, let's be frank—it doesn't always materialize that way. If your business isn't living up to your (or others') expectations, this isn't the end of the world. I will be honest, that sucks, no lie. Starting your own business is rewarding, but it is hard work and it is different work. If you are coming from corporate America, used to having back-end and staff support, only to find yourself responsible for nearly everything, that is jarring. Suddenly, HR, IT, AP, and every other job responsibility under the sun falls in your lap. Or it may be true that despite your best efforts and your best-laid plans, entrepreneurship isn't at all what you expected, or the business isn't as successful as projected. That is why flexibility in business (and in life, quite honestly) is a must. You must be open to change. You must be open to hearing other people's ideas and inputs.

Listen, in life, we are not going to "win" at everything we do.

Bill Gates and Steve Jobs weren't successful on their initial endeavors right out of the gate. If you are passionate about your project or service, try again. But try again after you have done your research on why the business didn't work, then retool, restructure or release it from there.

You may need to be flexible with your original plan. It is entirely possible that your business or business plan may transform into something else right before your eyes. As you share your vision with people to raise capital, meet with vendors or other interested parties (after they've signed your NDA, of course), the plan for your business may morph. I can say from experience, be open to changes. We often think we have the "best" plan or the "perfect vision" only to realize that we can't see the forest for the trees, and our great plan needs some work. Technology changes and globalization mean things move and morph at record speed, which may render a plan, app, platform or service obsolete— or, at the very least, changed. In the words of Deborah Day, "Flexibility requires an open mind and a welcoming of new alternatives." These are words to live by in business.

While my law firm has been successful, I have trod down many an entrepreneurial path, where some businesses were lucrative and others just weren't.

Case in point: I came up with what I knew was *the best* travel show idea on TV. I even got a development deal with the same company that produces *Expedition Unknown*, and with my 83 countries traveled, tourism boards in my back pocket, and a host of travel content articles I'd written for publications (that you can still google—hint, hint), you couldn't tell me I wasn't going to be the next Anthony Bourdain. (Minus the tragic ending, of course.) I knew it in my bones—this show where I was going to be travelling the world, producing content that would allow me to become a full-time content producer and on-camera talent, and getting paid talent and producer fees in the process.

Till every network passed!

You read that right. Okay, maybe not every network. But

every network the production company and their agents pitched it to. The feedback: with all this free travel content, why would a network pay anyone to put a show together? The networks simply weren't investing tons of money in travelogues (as we call them in TV land). My reply was, because there is no show like this one (and there still isn't) and it was a damn good idea. Which it was. But what matters is your customer, the buyer. And in this case, the networks weren't buying it.

In order to decide what your viable options are, you need to take a look at what went wrong. Perform a post-mortem on the business. Hold a focus group. Look at your goals and objectives. Did you accomplish those? Were they too lofty? Look at your product or service offered. How did you market your business? Was your product everything you had envisioned for the marketplace? This is the opportunity to take that deep dive and be brutally honest about your execution and your expectation.

I did just that when my show didn't get picked up. I emailed the production company and wanted to schedule a meeting to get some feedback. Was it our pitch, our reel? Was it me? They were gracious enough to give us feedback and hooked us up with their agent so we could do that post-mortem. It's always good to know what went wrong or why the potential customer isn't buying; we retooled, and even then it didn't get picked up. We send the reel out every now and then, but when Covid came around, we put our travel show on the shelf indefinitely, where it sits to this day.

You can always change course. And it bears mentioning that an LLC can be "recycled," as it can be formed for "any lawful purpose," so you don't have to shut it down if you change your business. Just remember to update your operating agreement in writing, and to amend any members or managers with the state. Of course, if you do dissolve your LLC, you must properly dissolve the entity, which includes paying any outstanding company debts. I still have my LLC I formed for my travel show, and am using that for various non-legal projects I'm involved in.

A corporation is a bit trickier to recycle. When you incorporate, you must specify your corporation's general objectives in the articles of incorporation. Some states allow a very vague business purpose description, while other states require more specificity. Look into your state's specifics, because if you don't adhere to the formation correctly, your application is likely to be rejected and sent back for clarification. Again, if you dissolve, you must wrap up your corporation, which includes dissolving the entity with the state and paying the corporate debts.

Be open. If the market has shifted so your company is no longer viable, or if your idea just isn't panning out, you may want to consider getting a job, full- or part-time, to supplement your income. If, after all of this, you simply want to throw in the towel, go for it. There is nothing wrong with that. Entrepreneurship is hard work and admittedly not for everyone, so if you have tried, were not successful, and want to go back to a day job, go for it. Eighty percent of small businesses may "survive" the first year, but only around half of those will survive five years. So, a lot of people end up leaving this chapter of their lives behind. At least you tried, which is more than a lot of people can say.

Chapter 4

RESOURCES AND FUNDING

"Money's a horrid thing to follow, but a charming thing to me."

— Henry James

NOW THAT YOUR business plan is written and your corporate entity formed, it's time to talk about funding. The good news is that there's plenty of money out there for small businesses and start-ups, you just have to know where to look. The JOBS Act (Jumpstart Our Business Startups Act) enacted in 2012 by President Obama has eased some of the onerous securities filings and regulations imposed on funding startups, thus making money more readily available. Title III of the Act, known as the crowdfunding exemption, has been very effective in stimulating investments in small American businesses by permitting companies to crowdfund (or gather) money from large numbers of non-accredited investors—a practice previously prohibited by SEC regulations. VC firms and angel investors are designed to provide investments in companies with an unpredictable cash flow and not much brand impact, so unique start-ups may get some funding from those sources. On the banking front, the Obama Administration eased lending restrictions and fostered a healthy economy, which has spurred small business borrowing. Let's examine these money options and where to find them.

A. CROWDFUNDING

This recent phenomenon is just what it sounds like—the ability to raise money from a large number of people. Previously, SEC regulations required stringent oversight and financial disclosure from "accredited investors": those making over $200,000 annually per person or $300,000 per couple over the previous two tax years; or those who have a net worth of over $1,000,000, excluding their primary residence. The JOBS Act loosened these regulations and allowed companies to raise money through a funding portal from anonymous investors. The portal you choose will depend on whether you are offering investors rewards or equity (ownership) in your company. In either scenario, crowdfunding rules only permit companies or individuals to raise money for specific products or projects, not for general operating revenue.

It's important to know that there are different types of crowdfunding, and not all crowdfunding is created equal. Each type has different ownership opportunities, as well as different fundraising limits. In order to optimize your chances at a successful funding campaign, you have to understand the differences and benefits of each type.

1. **Reward Funding**: Where the company offers perks or something of value to investors versus offering a return on their investment. In this scenario, there are virtually no rules regarding what kind of incentives to offer investors. From a personal delivery of the college student's home-cooked chili in exchange for funding his culinary quest, to a "thank you" on an artist's new album—you name it, the rewards offered are fair game. This is the least costly way to raise capital, and since there are very few requirements or disclosures, it is a great option for a company to fund research and development, a company's specific service or project, or raise an initial round of cash when a company might not meet all the requirements for a bank loan.

Kickstarter, Indiegogo and GoFundMe are some of the more popular portals for reward-based crowdfunding. Whether your non-profit is looking to raise money, or you are a podcaster or YouTuber looking to raise money, there are portals tailored to specific projects, so check online to see if there's an existing portal geared toward your desired service or project. One benefit of choosing a portal with your target-based audience is that you have a built-in, engaged community who may be more likely to invest in your project since they're familiar with and interested in your product or service.

You can raise any amount, from $1,000 to $100,000, by posting your campaign or story with a crowdfunding portal, which takes a portion of the proceeds (typically 7% to 12%). It is important to know that each portal operates differently with respect to releasing funds, so read the fine print. For example, Kickstarter doesn't release money if you don't meet your goal, whereas Indiegogo allows you to fund your project even if you don't meet your ask, but you will pay an increased fee for this option.

A successful campaign depends on a successful pitch. You should engage the viewer with a compelling story and communicate frequently with your target audience to incentivize them to invest. You have a limited amount of time to raise funds, so make a well-planned initial push and engage with your audience often.

2. **Equity Funding**: This is just like it sounds. The investor receives stock or shares in your company as a return on their investment. Governed by Title II of the JOBS Act, equity funding allows companies to raise an unlimited amount of money from an unlimited number of accredited investors. Recently, Title III of the JOBS Act takes this a step further by broadening the playing field for equity funding, allowing entrepreneurs to seek up to $1,000,000 from unaccredited investors through crowdfunding.

Although the SEC has eased rules and regulations on equity crowdfunding, they have not eliminated them completely. And unlike reward funding, you do have to file at least two forms and disclosures with the SEC. You must prepare a "Form C," which requires basic information about your company and the terms that govern the amount of money you are seeking to raise. You must also provide your company's financial statements to potential investors. The financial disclosures vary depending on your fundraising goals. If you're seeking $100,000 or less, you must provide certified financial statements executed by a company officer and your company's tax returns. If your ask is between $100,000 and $500,000, these disclosures must be verified by a CPA. And if you're raising over $500,000, these financials must be audited by a CPA if this is the company's first time selling securities under Regulation CF. While companies are not required to provide these audited financials on an ongoing basis, they must provide investors with annual reports and file these with the SEC, as well as post on the company's website. These filings provide investors with much-needed disclosure and transparency regarding their potential investment in the company, of which they now have some financial ownership.

B. SMALL BUSINESS ADMINISTRATION LOANS AND PROGRAMS

Many start-ups and new businesses don't have the credit history to secure a traditional bank loan. The Small Business Administration (SBA) has designed a number of lending programs to assist in funding your small business. The SBA doesn't directly provide loans; instead, they fund loans through local banks. So, if you have a relationship with a particular bank, think about making that your first stop when seeking financing. Irrespective of where you apply, it is still a bank loan, which means you must meet financial criteria and fill out several forms to qualify, but the forms and disclosures aren't too onerous.

There are various types of loans offered by the SBA, and each has different applications and filing requirements. Take a look around the SBA website (SBA.gov) to decide which loan best suits your needs. I have highlighted a few of the most common below.

1. **SBA Microloan**: Available to small businesses and some not-for-profit child care centers seeking $50,000 or less in funding. According to the SBA, the average Microloan is $13,000. As of the date this book was published, there was a six-year maximum repayment term, and interest rates ranged from 8% to 13%. Proceeds may be used for operating costs, to purchase inventory, supplies or equipment for your company, but may not be used to pay off creditors or purchase real estate. You can obtain a Microloan from community-based organizations, and you may be required to attend a business training program in order to obtain your loan.

2. **General Loan (7(a))**: The 7(a) loan is available for businesses seeking up to $5 million in funding (with no minimum loan amount). The associated fees are based on the amount guaranteed by the SBA rather than the total amount of the loan guaranteed by the bank. This program offers both fixed and variable rates; interest rates are negotiated directly between the local lender and the applicant.

    Note: There is a fairly detailed application process associated with 7(a) loans. In short, the SBA wants to assess your loan request and gather information about the applicant and any principals, including their creditworthiness, use of loan proceeds, and criminal offenses, if any. You begin by filling out the SBA Loan Application (Form 1919), which you can obtain online. The principals must submit a Personal Background and Financial Statement—Forms 912 and 413, respectively. You must also submit Business Certificates and Licenses and the applicants' income tax returns. (After all, if you can't run your own personal business and pay those taxes, what hope does the bank have in getting repayment on their loan?) You will also be required to submit the applicant and principals' résumés, business overview and history (which is another compelling reason to get your Business Plan intact, as we talked about in Chapter 1).

The company may use the 7(a) loan proceeds to establish a new business, expand an existing business, or purchase a new business. The proceeds may also be used to fund operating costs, as well as purchase inventory, supplies and/or equipment for your company. Unlike the Microloan, 7(a) proceeds may be used to purchase real estate and land, and you may use this to refinance existing debt under certain circumstances. The proceeds, however, may not be used to effectuate a change of ownership, repay owners for their loans to the company, or pay delinquent state or federal taxes.

3. **Disaster Loans**: If the government declares a disaster in your state and county ("Disaster Area"), and your business has suffered economic damage, you may apply to the SBA for an Economic Industry Disaster Loan ("EIDL"). This loan may provide up to $2 million to help your business pay for real property, machinery and equipment, inventory, to make business improvements or assistance. The EIDL works independently of other loans, insurance and other federal assistance available, such as FEMA monies. The EIDL provides relief irrespective of whether your business has suffered physical damage and is designed to provide assistance to restore your business economically as if the disaster had never happened. The loan is based on the disaster's economic impact on the business and is generally reserved for those businesses that are unable to obtain monies elsewhere. The terms are favorable. As of this book's publication date, interest rates were locked at 4%, with 30-year repayment terms.

There is also the Business Physical Damage Disaster Loan,

which is another $2 million loan available to your small business by the SBA. This loan, however, works very differently than the EIDL, in that your business must have suffered physical damage from the disaster. A Business Physical Damage Disaster Loan is intended to supplement insurance proceeds that will offset the physical damage sustained by the business. Like the EIDL, these loans may be used to purchase real property, machinery and equipment, inventory, and make improvements. Interest rates vary between 4% and 8%, depending on the business' ability to obtain credit elsewhere. Repayment terms may extend as long as 30 years.

C. ANGEL INVESTORS

Typically, "angels" (as they are sometimes called) are private investors who invest up to $500,000 from personal funds into new businesses in exchange for an equity stake in your company. Think *Shark Tank*—one of my fave shows, by the way. I think all entrepreneurs can learn volumes from the sharks. As angel investors are not banks, nor are they lending the company money, the risk/reward ratio is higher. Often the investment is in exchange for a 25%-50% equity stake in the business.

When looking to invest in companies, angels look for strong management teams who are visionaries, with clear and concise business plans. They look to invest in companies that have the ability to change the existing landscape or solve a problem for the consumer, even if that product is novel. In exchange, the angel investors are generally savvy and forward-thinking, and can bring years of expertise to your company, increasing the odds that it will flourish. A Harvard Business School study found that companies backed by angel investors stayed in business longer, had higher yields on their investments, and a higher growth percentage than those backed by traditional loans.

Not for nothing, but Google and Costco—both of which eventually became game changers—are two examples of companies which were successful at obtaining angel investors, and there are too many success stories to name from *Shark Tank*. An angel's guidance, as you can see, is often invaluable for your business.

D. VENTURE CAPITAL MONIES

Venture capital firms are generally made up of investment banks and wealthy investors who pool funds to provide funding to businesses that cannot secure funding or raise capital through traditional means of bank loans, traditional debt or equity financing. Venture capital is primarily for businesses that are in attractive markets (usually some form of technology) that have grown quickly in the past or have otherwise demonstrated a high growth potential in the area the venture capitalist firm is seeking to invest.

Unlike angel investors, venture capitalists generally aren't early investors; rather, they invest in a company after an initial round of seed financing. But like angels, these investors know the field, so they provide advice and direction in exchange for equity ownership. But the end goal is enough growth to expand and make the company attractive with an eye towards an exit, usually in the form of an initial public offering. Uber and Airbnb are successful companies that received venture capital monies and went on to greatness.

VC monies are difficult to come by, so this shouldn't be a source of funding you hang your hat on. According to the SBA, about 600,000 new businesses are started annually, and venture capitalists only invest in an average of about 300 companies per year. If you are looking to raise money from a venture capital firm, there are many articles and references that go into the different stages of investment. But since the odds are so slim that the average entrepreneur will garner VC monies, it's best not to muddy the waters too much, as other funding is more readily available to entrepreneurs and freelancers.

E. GRANTS AND OTHER FUNDING PROGRAMS

If you look closely and peel back enough layers, you will find there's an abundance of funding available in the form of grants, contests and festival prizes (especially if you are in filmmaking) for which you can apply. Women-owned and minority-owned businesses in particular have several organizations that set aside money to fund start-up and small business initiatives. The following are some useful resources for "free" money:

Grants.gov, powered by the Small Business Administration and U.S. Department of Commerce, is a useful website and search engine where you can search over 1,000 different types of grants from 26 different agencies. It has a user-friendly interface packed with useful information, including a definitive breakdown of various grants, how to determine one's eligibility, and several other menus and sections to aid and assist you on your journey to finding and applying for federal grant monies.

1. The Commerce Department also runs the Minority Business Development Agency, which connects minority businesses to funding agencies, federal contracting opportunities, and other funding options in the marketplace. Check out mbda.gov/blogger/export-finance/listing for updates and spend time on their website to access resources and updates.

2. The SBA has created the 8(a) Business Development Program, which is the most lucrative program to assist "small, disadvantaged groups" obtain government contracts. Although the application is time consuming and extremely onerous, the payoff and assistance to your business can potentially be huge. The Program is available to companies that are 51% or more owned by a socially and economically disadvantaged individual(s) (e.g., Black, Hispanic, Alaskan, Native American). Other program requirements include that the applicant

have experience in government contracting, must be an American citizen, have a personal net worth of less than $250,000, can demonstrate a potential for success and a few other stipulations found on the SBA website, where you may apply for the 8(a) program. You must first be certified as a "Small Business" by the SBA, which is pretty straightforward by applying on their website. If you are selected for the 8(a) designation, you may stay in the program for a maximum of nine years, and your company gains a shot at "sole source" (not out for bid) government contracts. The government's goal is to set aside up to five percent of all contracts to "small, disadvantaged businesses" each year, so if you meet the criteria, it is definitely worth the application. The program provides a program specialist to help you navigate the federal contracts, and your business can also receive technical, business, and marketing assistance and executive counseling through the 8(a) program.

3. Similarly, the SBA has a certification process for Women-Owned Small Businesses (WOSBs) and Economically Disadvantaged WOSBs (EDWOSBs) businesses, which is designed to help disenfranchised groups gain a level footing in business. The requirements are similar to those of the 8(a) Program, so check online at SBA.gov to qualify and apply for the loan. Likewise, if you're a female-owned and minority-owned businesses, you should register with the appropriate state and federal agencies. These affiliations allow your company to avail itself of monies similar in nature to the SBA programs, where you apply for grants and programs in your particular industry that are earmarked for that particular affiliation.

Up until now, we've talked cautionary tales in your pursuit of excellence, but now we're going to turn our focus to balance over Tea Time.

TEA TIME

The Art of Saying "No"

"Only the (wo)man who says no is free."

— Herman Melville

ONE OF THE biggest misconceptions about entrepreneurship (and life) is that you *have* to be busy and stay busy…constantly busy. If you aren't working yourself to the point of exhaustion, you are not "really working," on the fast track to falling flat on your face! Nothing could be further from the truth. I recently saw a meme going around social media that implored us to "Stop the Glorification of Busy." Yes, Lord! If that is not a word that took me all the way to church, I don't know what is!

We'll talk about the importance of rest later on, but before you can get to the point of resting, you have to learn to say and embrace saying "no." You can't rest if you are constantly saying "yes" to everything. That is why it is important to recharge, and why you must get comfortable with saying no, setting boundaries and sticking to them. You have to respect your time, because people can "yes" you and your time to death. Then you end up being mad because you didn't want or have the time to do whatever it is "they" asked you to do.

There are a few core truths that will help you learn to say no and stick to it. Firstly, understand that *no* is a whole word! You don't owe anyone an explanation for why you don't want to do anything! If you have to take your kids to practice, or your dog (or in my case, the cats) to the vet, or you just need time to yourself, that is your business. Women in particular tend to overexplain (myself included!) and justify to other people why we can't do something. Stop that! A simple "thank you for thinking of me, but I have a prior commitment" will do just fine. So will: "Thanks, but I can't make it." That's it, end of discussion. Say it and stick to your *no*.

Secondly, learn to listen to your spirit, your inner self. If something doesn't feel good in your gut, it probably is not going to work out in the short or long run. When your first mind is filled with doubt about something, there is probably a reason. If you have to ask around, consult, think too long or hard about something, and you are already having doubts, proceed with caution. After you decide either way, look back, because hindsight is 20/20. We are learning to exercise that *no* muscle, which means checking in, taking the temperature of how you felt. Did it feel good to say no? Are you at peace? If so, then you made the right decision. Did you say yes? Are you feeling okay about it, or is your spirit off and you're in a corner at that event with a screwface?

Next is an old adage: As my grandmother used to say, "Every goodbye ain't gone!" Meaning that just because you are saying no to that particular invitation/event/client doesn't mean it can't take place at another time. We have to start looking at our interpersonal interaction as a reciprocal exchange of time and energy. Meaning, interactions have to work for both people. Ask yourself: "How will this benefit me?" When you stop and take stock, you might realize that you're probably doing more things than you really want or have time to do, and you are overcommitting yourself. If it is something you want to do, and it's beneficial to you, then ask yourself: "Does that time/date/place work for me?" For example, if you want to have that lunch, but don't want to do it on that day, suggest another day. "Thanks for the invitation for lunch. I can't make it on Monday, how about next

Wednesday?" You will be surprised at how many people will, when given a choice of no, not at all, or yes to another time, will choose another time that works for both people.

This is something that really took time and intentionality for me in order to get good at and comfortable doing—especially when I *really* wanted to do something, but it just didn't, at that time, work for me. Case in point: I recently had a production company contact me about doing a small talent gig for them. The day before the shoot, something came up on their end and they wanted to move my call time from 1:00 to 6:00, because of a glitch at the proposed filming location. A 6:00 p.m. start time on a Saturday (which was the only day that I could do it) was a hard pass for me, and I told them as much: "I'm sorry, but that isn't going to work for me." Period. Weekends are my only time off, and I have set boundaries about what I will and will not do, for how long, and when. As much as I wanted the opportunity, I was equally prepared to walk away from it. But given the opportunity, or the choice of losing it, I suggested we shoot at my house or on Sunday. For production reasons, they didn't want to do it initially, but understanding that my *no* wasn't going to change, they gracefully accommodated my schedule. They came to my house, we shot the segment, and I got them out of my house in time for my "me time" on Saturday night. Again, saying no and sticking to it took practice, and so did the confidence to speak up for myself. Once you realize that what is meant for you will never miss you, you will not only get comfortable, but you'll get to a place of peace with saying no.

The same principle applies to work and your services: learn to say no to the request for free services and know when to say no additional work or become comfortable walking away from something because the terms don't work for you. When thinking about taking on more work, just remember that more clients/orders/etc. do not necessarily mean that it will yield a bigger payout. If you have to hire more people, have no time, or the money you make will be going into third parties' pockets, or it's just not enough money to justify the work, learn to say no. It is quality over quantity. You will get to the point in your business when you have the ability to turn away new customers. Of course, if you want to grow bigger, that is fine as well, but every entrepreneurial endeavor doesn't have to turn into some ginormous production or a big business to yield benefits. At Bonner Law, PC, we are a small but mighty bunch, and we get it done. Just ask my clients.

Recently, I had a studio come to me about working on their film. It was a very big and lucrative project, and one I wanted to be involved in. *But…* But for the fact that it pushed up against principal photography on a TV show I was already working on. The insanely quick pace of work during the production push sometimes leaves very little time to attend to my sanity, let alone other projects. I know how I work best and under which circumstances, and their proposed time frame and the amount of work they needed was a lot. I knew that if I accepted the film, I would be pushing my time and sanity envelope. But they really wanted me on the film, and eventually I gave in. I agreed that I would represent them with very specific parameters that I, of course, outlined in the engagement letter.

Remember that gut check I mentioned earlier? You know when your first mind is telling you what you know you should do, but you do the opposite? Well, that was me. I hesitated about taking the job because of time constraints but eventually gave into the project. I went against my first thought, and I should have trusted that feeling. All I can say is, thank goodness for the lawyer's engagement/retainer letter. Remember that from Chapter 2? What happened: The scope of services the clients *really* wanted were vastly different than we negotiated and the fee we settled on. Turns out, they were so far off, I would go so far as to say they knowingly misrepresented the nature and scope of work and wanted twice the amount of work for half the amount of money. If they had been forthcoming, my rate and availability would have *far* exceeded what we agreed on. No amount of money is enough money if it's not sufficient to cover the time and work involved. Think about it: I am losing money on this project to help you make money. That's a *no*! Ultimately, I said no and resigned from the project days into it. It felt good to walk away even though it was a substantial amount of money, and I felt just fine about it.

Time is a precious commodity. That is the one thing we can't make more of, so value it! If you don't value your own time, you can't expect other people to value yours. #JustSayNO

Chapter 5

HIRING EMPLOYEES AND INDEPENDENT CONTRACTORS

*"Life is the continuous adjustment of
internal relations to external relations."*

— Herbert Spencer

NOW THAT YOU'VE successfully established your corporate formalities, you may be ready to start staffing your business. While many people may not pay particular attention to the formalities of engaging individuals, *how* someone is engaged is important from a benefits perspective. If you actually employ someone, they may (depending on your company's size) be eligible for paid time off and other benefits, such as unemployment. If someone is hired on an independent contractor basis (e.g., freelancers, gig workers), that relationship does not require the payment of benefits, as they are considered to be self-employed. There are also different tax implications for companies hiring employees and utilizing independent contractors, so it is important to properly classify your workers. Failure to properly qualify people can cost you money in taxes and penalties owed to the IRS, state and local taxing authorities, civil penalties and other implications.

With so much at stake with the correct classification, you need to be clear about the role the proposed worker will be playing at the company and how they will be managed prior to deciding to classify someone as an independent contractor versus an employee. To make matters worse, not only are there not any clear-cut rules to determine who's an employee and who can be classified as an independent contractor, but the rules vary depending on the governing body interpreting the classification. The IRS, Department of Labor, state and the federal government each have their own classifications. State and federal labor laws often conflict, and federal employment and labor laws require that the law that yields the worker the greatest benefit controls.

Let's take a look at what it means for your business to engage an employee or an independent contractor.

Hiring Employees: Plain and simple, employing people costs your business money—money that you don't have to pay if your business is utilizing independent contractors. The U.S. Department of Labor states that employers are "legally required to provide benefits to workers and their families with retirement income and medical care, mitigate economic hardship resulting from loss of work and disability, and cover liabilities resulting from workplace injuries and illnesses." The IRS agrees, so one thing is for certain, and two for sure: classifying a worker as an employee mandates that employers pay payroll taxes. Although contrary to popular belief, employers are not required to give paid time off and other fringe benefits, employers are required to carry worker's compensation and pay into unemployment insurance for employees, and pay other taxes on employees, which increases the cost of hiring an employee.

As always, the government is in your business, and there are legal governmental requirements that employers must comply with prior to any hire. Every employee is required to submit an I-9 form, establishing the employee's eligibility in the United States. Additionally, the employer must provide the employee with a W4 form (irs.gov/pub/irs-pdf/fw4.pdf) used to document the amount of withholdings that the employer must deduct from the employee's check. The employee bases these deductions on their filing status, number of dependents, and any anticipated tax credits. The employer must file W2 forms with the IRS for each employee by January 31, which evidences the amount of taxes withheld from the employee's check, and the employee will then file this form with her taxes.

Next, you must decide whether to pay your employees an hourly or a salaried wage. If you opt for the hourly wages, you are subjected to federal and state minimum wage laws and are required to pay the higher wage requirement of the two. Irrespective of whether the employee is salaried or hourly, the employer is required to pay Social Security taxes and Medicare (FICA) taxes (currently 7.65 percent of the employee's wages), as well as Federal Unemployment (FUTA) taxes (currently 6 percent of the first $7,000 of employee's wages). The employer also pays State unemployment taxes (SUTA), which vary by state, on each employee each time you run payroll. These fund your state's unemployment fund, which pays benefits to employees in certain instances of termination or downsizing.

One cost benefit for small businesses is that, contrary to popular misconceptions, employers with fewer than 50 employees are not *required* to provide healthcare, or unpaid medical or family leave. However, there are federal tax credits available to small companies that offer healthcare plans to their employees. Companies are not required to provide retirement packages or other benefits, but typically employers do provide at least paid time off and/or healthcare as part of the benefits package as incentives to attract employees. The cost of the employee benefits packages can quickly add up and increase your financial bottom line upwards of 30% of the employee's compensation package.

If you are a small business and can't afford those benefits, get creative. Some ways to incentivize your employees include allowing employee flex time, permitting employees to work remotely on a certain number of days per week, providing lunches, or even childcare for your employees' kids. There are no limit to the creative ways to incentivize employees; and this is especially true in the pandemic, so ask around or put on your thinking cap.

Finally, although not required, you should memorialize the employee offer in writing. An offer letter should clearly and specifically set forth the conditions of employment, if any, including whether employment is contingent upon references or passing a background and/or drug test. The letter should also include the start date, job title and description of duties, location, hours (full- or part-time), compensation, pay periods, employee's benefits (if any) and when the benefits kick in. Of course, don't forget to sign the letter and make sure you get and retain a copy signed by the employee.

Hiring employees also invokes several legal issues that you need to be aware of, because any time you terminate an employee, it must be done in accordance with the law. Even with an at-will employee (one you may terminate for any reason or no reason at all), their termination must be within the legal confines of termination. For example, you can't terminate an employee for pregnancy or because the employee is "too old." It is illegal to fire an employee based on their race, religion, gender, national origin, disability, pregnancy or age (if the person is 40 years or older). Valid reasons for terminating an employee include misconduct, poor performance, a valid reason according to a state or federal statute, or redundancy (change in job's location, business is closing, the employer requires fewer workers).

An illegal termination of an employee may result in the employee bringing a wrongful termination suit against the employer. But many terminations fall in the grey area, which adds another layer of complexity to the situation. What if your pregnant employee just flat out isn't performing well? What if she has a lackadaisical attitude towards the job and a snippy attitude with your customers? Those grey areas are reasons for pause and could open up a wrongful termination suit from the terminated employee. The former employee could assert that her termination is due to her pregnancy and not poor performance and attitude. Hire an experienced employment attorney who can help you navigate the murky employment waters. I also strongly advise you to keep detailed employee records documenting work performance and attendance of each and every employee.

So, the employee's been terminated. Now what? In certain instances, an employee may be entitled to collect unemployment benefits. The terminated employee may have valid reasons for seeking unemployment such as downsizing, getting laid off or quitting due to employer misconduct. If the employee collects unemployment, that money comes from the FUTA and SUTA payroll taxes paid into by the employer.

If the former employee is seeking unemployment benefits, she files a claim with the state's unemployment board, which sends a letter to the former employer. The employer may contest it or not. If you are contesting the claim, you need to show proof to dispute the claim, which is why keeping copious records on all your employees is a good idea. "Vengeance is mine," sayeth the terminated employee. I've seen some egregious claims filed in instances where that terminated employee had absolutely no leg to stand on contesting termination, yet still had the gall to file an unemployment claim. You need to keep tight records to overcome and combat these often-bogus claims. If you fail to contest the claim, or if your contested claim is rejected, then the claim will be paid. The state will "charge" your unemployment account, and your FUTA and SUTA taxes will go up. Think of the increase as a way to "pay back into" the unemployment pot, even though you already paid vis-à-vis their employment taxes.

An employer has a lot of financial and legal responsibilities attached to hiring employees which simply aren't an issue with independent contractors. So, let's dig into that and shed some light on the differences.

Hiring Independent Contractors. It is much less costly to your bottom line to hire people as independent contractors, because the employer isn't paying those payroll taxes which quickly add up. Because the state and local governments aren't collecting the tax revenue from employers, the government has really cracked down on who and what constitutes an independent contractor. However, as mentioned, there is no one definition of what constitutes an "independent contractor" amongst the states, or federal and various agencies.

In determining the status of the worker, the IRS provides guidelines under the 20-Factor Test to take into consideration. A worker does not have to meet all 20 factors to qualify as an employee or independent contractor, and no single factor is decisive in determining a worker's status. Generally, the more control a company exercises over who, what, when, where and how the work is performed, and the extent to which the worker is under the control of the company, the more likely the worker is classified as an employee as opposed to an independent contractor. For the most part, the 20 factors use common law rules to classify an individual as an independent contractor or an employee using three buckets: Behavioral Control, Financial Control and the Type of Relationship between the parties.

- **Behavioral Control:** An employer usually dictates when, where and how the work is performed by the worker and looks at whether the employer trains the employee to perform the work or achieve the desired results. An independent contractor, on the other hand, is free to perform the work on his or her own schedule and times designated, as long as the deadline is met, and doesn't receive any training.

- **Financial Control:** This step looks at whether the employer reimburses expenses, covers supplies and materials needed for the job's completion, and how the worker is paid. An independent contractor is responsible for the costs of doing business, and is not reimbursed for overhead, computer, meals, and other reasonable and customary expenses in the ordinary course of business. However, it is important to note that independent contractors may in some instances be reimbursed for meals and travel if traveling on behalf of the job, but those general overhead expenses fall squarely on the independent contractor.

- **Type of Relationship:** What is the relationship between the parties? An employer provides the worker with paid vacations, extends benefits such as health coverage and pension plans to the worker. An independent contractor will not receive any of the job's fringe benefits. This is an absolute and providing any type of worker benefits in this category will lend itself to any employer/employee relationship.

If, after reviewing the three categories, you're still unsure about your classification, you can file a Form SS-8 (Determination of Worker Status for Purposes of Federal Employment Taxes and Income Tax Withholding) with the IRS for a determination of the worker's status. Be forewarned: the wait for a determination is long. Sometimes it takes up to six months for a determination, which is why it's always best to consult a lawyer with specific questions regarding your specific situation.

The Department of Labor has been in flux over what constitutes an independent contractor, as former President Trump relaxed some of the more stringent rules, and the current Biden Administration reinstating rules has created a yo-yo effect for the employer trying to get the classification right. As of this book's publication date, what's apparent is that more states are extending employee benefits to independent contractors and codifying the laws regarding the rules, imposing harsh penalties for the company if not adhered to.

For the most part, the legal factors and tests used to determine whether a worker is an independent contractor varies widely from state to state. California, by far the most employee-friendly state, now requires *all* workers to be classified as an employee under Assembly Bill 5 ("AB5"), which codifies the court decision handed down under *Dynamex Operations West v. Superior Court of Los Angeles* (2018). That decision mandates a worker be classified as an employee unless the business can establish all three of the following criteria, otherwise known as the ABC Test. Under the ABC Test, the employer must demonstrate a) that the worker is not under the direct control of the company, b) that the worker performs work for the company outside of the company's usual line of business, and c) that the worker is performing the job duties of their regularly established trade, occupation or business.

The first prong requires the employer to show that the worker is indeed a freelancer, and truly independent of the company's control and input. The worker must be able to set her own schedule, charge prices as she determines, hire and determine personnel necessary for the work independent of the company, and regulate her own work flow and the manner in which the services are provided.

The second prong stipulates that the worker must perform work that is outside of the normal course of business for the company. Meaning you can't run, for example, a nail salon business and hire a host of nail technicians who work at your business and classify them as independent contractors. In that instance, the business owner owns a salon and all the workers in the salon are providing the work that is in the normal course of the business you are running.

The third prong of the ABC Test turns on whether the worker is independently engaged in the line of work or trade that she is providing for the company. Meaning that the worker is able to freely deliver those same services on the open market for others without restriction from the company.

Only in instances where the business can demonstrate that the worker can meet all of the prongs of the ABC Test may she be classified as an independent contractor. The controversial AB5 bill also requires all *existing* independent contractor workers who don't meet each of the criteria to be reclassified as employees. The employer must now pay the employer taxes (social security, Medicare, federal and state unemployment taxes) on the revenue paid to the worker and, depending on the circumstances, could be subject to state and local penalties.

This reclassification has caused an uproar in California, as it undermines companies' ability to hire contractors. But it raised much needed revenue for the state, as companies are now forced into paying state employment taxes on the workers. The ABC Test came under further scrutiny because of the seeming arbitrary selection of professions which may retain their independent contractor status. Travel agents working for an agency were exempt, but the nail technician who works in the same capacity is not. Professional service providers, such as doctors, lawyers, architects and engineers, are still exempt in certain instances.

The California bill is being amended on a regular basis. As of this book's publication date, AB5 was amended to include studio and live musicians as exemptions under the bill. Proposition 22 was also passed, which allowed a carve-out for gig workers at companies like Uber, Lyft and DoorDash—permitting these app-based transportation workers and delivery drivers to adopt industry-specific wage rules. So, check back regularly to determine the applicability of your profession if you're employing workers in California.

It's been said, "As California goes, so goes the nation," and it seems the prevailing trend in many states is following California in placing stricter mandates in what constitutes an independent contractor relationship. As of this book's publication date, Connecticut, Delaware, Illinois, Indiana, Massachusetts, Nebraska, Nevada, New Hampshire, New Jersey, New York, Vermont, Washington and West Virginia have all adopted the ABC Test.

Now that you have a bit more clarity on the classification of the workers you intend to hire, you need to make sure your paperwork is airtight. We discussed this in the previous Tea Time; this paperwork should clearly set out the nature and parameters of your working relationship. Most independent contractor agreements specifically outline and disclaim, not surprisingly, the ABC Test considerations.

For independent contractors and freelancers, the key provision in the paperwork should clearly disclaim benefits offered and put the tax onus on the contractor. The key provision should read something along the following lines:

Independent Contractor: Nothing herein contained shall be construed to constitute the parties to this Agreement as partners or as joint venturers, or either as agent of the other, or as employer and employee. Consultant's relationship to the Company during the Term shall only be that of an independent contractor and Consultant shall perform all Services pursuant to this Agreement as an independent contractor. Nothing in this Agreement, however, will be deemed to constitute Consultant's employees as agents, or employees of the Company. Neither Consultant nor the Company shall incur any indebtedness, enter into any undertaking or make any commitment in the other party's name or purport to act on the other party's behalf, except with the other party's prior written approval. Moreover, the Company has no obligation to withhold and/or pay any income, employment or other taxes, and Consultant specifically holds Company harmless from and against Contractor's failure to pay taxes on Compensation earned hereunder. Contractor shall have no claim against the Company hereunder or otherwise for vacation pay, sick leave, retirement benefits, social security, worker's compensation, health or disability benefits, unemployment insurance benefits, or employee benefits of any kind. Neither Consultant nor Consultant's employees may cite services under this Agreement in support of any claim to be an employee of the Company for the purpose of claiming any statutory or common law benefit.

Similar tax paperwork is needed for independent contractors. The contractor will need to fill out the Form I-9 to establish the contractor's ability to be hired in the United States. The company will collect a W9 with the contractor's tax identification number to report the income paid to the independent contractor to the IRS, and similar to providing the employee with a W2, the company will provide the contractor with a 1099 at the end of the year evidencing the amount of compensation paid to the contractor.

TEA TIME

Becoming a Great Leader

"Give a man a fish and you feed him for a day; teach a man to fish and you feed him for a lifetime."

— Maimonides

WHETHER YOU ARE hiring employees or independent contractors, you have people working with you and you are responsible for their output. That responsibility makes you the *boss*. Being a boss is one thing, but being an effective leader is something that good bosses strive for. Becoming an effective leader is a challenge and a chore in itself. You are balancing: you're trying to run a business, get the most out of your workers and have a rapport with them, while building a professional (i.e., not too chummy) relationship. You can end up trying to please everyone, and in the end, you may please no one, not even yourself. How do you keep that balance and lead your team effectively? Therein lies the challenge. But I believe that there is a secret sauce to becoming an effective leader.

Never forget that you're managing human resources, i.e., people, and those people who work for you can make or break the company. Therefore, it is important to get to know your people. Get to know their temperament and their skills, as well as their weaknesses. When hiring, it is important to be clear about the skills needed for the position and seek out people who possess those strengths. If you are inheriting people, make an extra effort to get to know them, to ensure they are tasked for the position that they're working in. You don't want to have a Grumpy Gail answering the phone or otherwise interacting with customers. But if Gail can balance a spreadsheet, maybe she's better suited for a position in the back office. When a new boss comes in, it's not uncommon that there's often a shakeup at the company, as the new boss takes stock to ensure she has the right people in the right positions. People are your most precious resources.

While getting to know people, you may be tempted to try to become friends with your employees. In a word: don't. I am not suggesting that you take a standoff-ish approach, but on the other hand, most effective leaders will tell you it is better to keep a professional distance between you and your workers. You know the old adage: familiarity breeds contempt, and that is indeed a truism in business.

Monica, my executive assistant, has worked with me for 10 years. She holds the keys to my queendom: she knows all my clients, has my personal and company banking information. She can recite my social security number, knows my mother's maiden name. You name it, she knows it. Essentially, Monica could take out a mortgage or open credit cards in my name, and I trust her implicitly. But we are not friends. We have a healthy respect for each other, and we even really like each other; we are friendly, but we aren't friends. We do not go out and socialize together, or yap on the phone like girlfriends. We have established healthy boundaries, which in turn yields a healthy working relationship. She knows my expectations, and she handles them. In turn, I pay her on time, without fail, for what she is hired to do. I respect her time and treat her fairly. It's transactional. Business is business, and it's best not to mix business with pleasure.

Although you don't have to become chummy with your workers to get the best from them, you don't have to be aloof or standoffish either. You can be interested in their families, hobbies, and get to know people, of course. But I definitely don't recommend befriending and hanging out on a regular basis with those who work for you, because it just muddies the waters. (I recommend this to every "boss," whether it is your company or not.) I have found that treating people with respect, rather than being someone's "friend," is the best way to get the most from your workers.

Now that you are on the road to effective leadership, you want to keep it that way. You want to continue to bring out the best in your employees. People are predisposed to point out the negative things and slow to point out the good; that's just human nature. But nothing is more of a morale killer than continuously pointing out the mistakes or what needs improvement. It's demoralizing and immediately puts people on the defensive. You want to team-build, not tear down. If you interview, and set your expectations upfront, and have *your* stuff in order, you should have the basis for a good worker. But getting acclimated is tough, and it takes time for people to learn how to do things your way. So naturally, there will be a learning curve and mistakes will invariably be made. But when correcting those mistakes, always start with the strengths, and then course-correct from there.

I am picky and have a certain way that I want to run my firm. I have high expectations of my employees and contractors. When Monica started with me, I had my lengthy assistant handbook which included sample correspondence, specific logs, every bit of information she needed on what to do and how to do it, all the way down to what verbiage to use when answering my phone and transferring calls. Even with all of that, we still had a few bumps in the road. But I knew that Monica was a good person and could be the employee that I needed. I knew she could catch on, with explanations and a little patience (which hadn't been my strong suit). I treated her with respect and had conversations, often difficult ones, about the way I wanted *my* business run. Relationships that are worth it often test your patience, and it is up to *you*, the effective leader, to set the tone and example of how to communicate, and the manner in which you like things done.

One last tip on becoming an effective leader, which is the premise of this entire book: make sure you have *your* stuff in order. Fish stinks from the head. You can't expect your workers to come in and do a job if you don't have a clear-cut definition of what the job entails and how to do it. They're employees, not mind readers. You need to have a roadmap, examples, forms and training materials. Half your battle is knowing where to go, but the devil is in the details on how to get there. And those details are your job. But if you are utilizing the tools in this book, you will definitely have the road map to boss up and become the effective leader you were meant to be.

Chapter 6

ESTABLISHING AND PROTECTING YOUR DOMAIN NAME AND WEBSITE

"Business today consists of persuading crowds."

— Gerald Stanley Lee

NOW THAT YOU'VE established your business *and* have secured (or are in the process of securing) funding, it's time to let the world know what you're up to! Think of your website as your coming out party, letting the world know you've arrived and showing them who you are, what your business is about, and how your business can benefit the world.

Think of your website as a way to market yourself and your business. In this virtual world, the first thing most people turn to is a website to learn about your product…and you. It doesn't have to have a lot of bells and whistles, color photos and dropdown menus. But it does need to show you and your product in the best possible light. Of all the people and businesses in the world, why should people choose *you*?

But before all that, of course, let's talk about the LegaliTEAS of your website. Firstly, the type of website you have will dictate what type of legal compliance and disclaimers you will need to include on your site. If you are simply designing a static website—where you are providing information only and not collecting any personal data—then simply register your domain name with any number of registration companies (GoDaddy, Google, Register.com), use their templates (or another easy provider, such as WordPress), and build a webpage. However, if you're collecting information from visitors, selling a product, allowing content posts from users, engaging in social interaction or a myriad of other transactions, you are going to need to protect yourself and be in compliance with the law, and there are certain disclaimers and policies you need to post.

PRIVACY POLICIES

A Privacy Policy is going to be the most important "small print" on your website. This keeps you in compliance with state and federal government regulations, something that neither entity (or consumers) takes lightly. Therefore, if you are collecting any "personal information" from visitors to your site, displaying ads or collecting analytics, you are required by law to display a Privacy Policy. This policy is a document on your website that discloses to each visitor what information you are collecting from them, how you plan to use this information, how the information is shared with third parties, how the website keeps the information private, and how to opt-out of data collection and emails. What entails "personal information" varies from state to state, but generally includes any collection of your name, email address, gender, ethnicity and birthdate. Depending on the site, they may ask for additional information such as your occupation, education, religion, political party, bank account or credit card information. Basically, the collection of just about any information from your visitors requires you by law to display a privacy policy.

California was one of the first states to mandate how companies collect and disclose the online collection of data. California's "Shine the Light" law, Civil Code section 1798.83, requires companies that do business with California residents to allow customers to either opt out of information sharing or make a detailed disclosure of how their personal information is shared for direct marketing purposes.

However, your company doesn't need to be located in California to fall under this law's jurisdiction; you simply need one visitor to your website from that state. If your business has fewer than 20 employees, or is a non-profit, your company is exempt, but it still doesn't hurt to include the language in your privacy policy. The language must include the verbiage "Your Privacy Rights" or "Your California Privacy Rights" on the homepage, with a link describing the customer's rights to request a no-cost way to receive (within 30 days) the disclosures, and a dedicated point of contact for the request. Failure to comply will result in a penalty of up to $500 per violation (increases to $3,000 if it's deemed "willful"), plus attorney's fees and costs.

Another law unique to California that affects the website's privacy provision is the California Consumer Privacy Act ("CCPA"). In summary, the advocate behind the ballot's initiative, which went into law on January 2, 2020, dubbed the Act "the right to know" and "the right to say no." The CCPA requires businesses that collect personal information to inform consumers of the categories of personal information to be collected and specify how (as in what areas and industries) your information will be used. The Act also requires companies to delete the user's data upon written notification. The CCPA applies to companies which conduct business in California and either 1) earns an annual revenue exceeding $25 million, 2) gathers data on more than 50,000 users, or 3) makes more than half its money off of user data. While this doesn't sound like it may be applicable to your company, it is easy to amass a database of 50,000 users, as the entrepreneur's goal is to sell to as many customers as possible. Since California leads the country in data privacy and routinely changes their requirements, adding this paragraph is generally a good idea for your company's site regardless. It's always better to be safe than sorry.

TERMS OF USE

The Terms of Use section (also known as "Terms of Service") is essentially the contract between you and your end user. If there is ever a dispute over how your site is used, and who owns the data and intellectual property that the user submits on the site, the Terms of Use will govern. This is where the courts will look in the event of a dispute between you and the user. To ensure you are properly protected, the Terms of Use should contain several key elements:

Ownership

This is an important section, as ownership is divided into two distinct buckets. There is your (the owner's) bucket that outlines your company's ownership of the intellectual property, data collected, and functionality of the site. There is also the ownership of the personal data as submitted, and any content that is submitted to the site by the user.

As the owner, you own all rights, title, and interest in and to any and all content *displayed* on the site, including the site's design, data, information, text, graphics, images, sound or video materials, designs, trademarks, service marks, trade names and URL. As the site owner, you obviously can't own the user's data. But you can and do own any lists derived from the owner's personal data. So, if your user is uploading content, the ownership or disclaimer of that user's data ownership should be outlined in this section.

COPPA Compliance

The Children's Online Privacy Protection Act (COPPA) is designed to protect the online collection of personal data of children under 13. This is particularly important if you are selling products or distributing content on your site, as this requires parental consent. If your site does collect data with parental consent, this data must be kept private and confidential. And you may not sell or aggregate this personal data that you have legally collected from users under 13.

Disclaimers

Since you don't have the time nor energy to police the site, you will want to make sure you have a section in the Terms where you disclaim the accuracy, integrity or quality of any third-party content on the site. Such content may include data, text, software, music, sound, photographs, graphics, video, messages, tags, or other materials on the site, whether publicly posted or privately transmitted.

Similarly, your Terms should also include a separate provision whereby you disclaim warranties and what we lawyers call "fitness for a particular purpose." As your website is providing general information, it is not tailored specifically for one user's particular needs. If your website provides advice, giving recipes, instructions, directions—quite frankly, any kind of information—you want to disclaim that your website is not addressing that user's particular needs on the site using this disclaimer. Many people are litigious, and there is no shortage of lawyers ("ambulance chasers") looking to make a quick buck off an aggrieved individual who claims that "I used your recipe, product, etc., and I was damaged/fell ill/worsened my condition, etc." Your Terms are your best offense to a great defense.

DMCA COMPLIANCE

The Safe Harbor provision of the Digital Millennium Copyright Act of 1998 (DMCA), 17 U.S.C. §512 et seq., can shield your business from liability in the event that you unknowingly have a third party infringing material posted by a user on your site. This is an important provision for your website, as it negates the company's need to police and verify user-submitted content. In the same regard, it also protects the copyright owner's right to have their infringed material removed from a website as long as the proper protocols are followed.

Under DMCA, the copyright holder sends written notice to the website owner or service provider requesting that they remove the infringing material. The Act sets forth several specific elements that must be set forth in a Takedown Notice, which includes a sworn statement identifying the material on the service provider's site, the infringed material's specific use on the site, contact information and other elements. If the Takedown Notice doesn't meet the requirements, the service provider may refuse the takedown request. Ultimately, even if all provisions are met, the takedown is discretionary. However, if the company fails to remove the infringing material, they lose the protection under the DMCA's Safe Harbor Act and can potentially be liable for copyright infringement.

Therefore, the Terms of Use on your website should include a statement that you have the right, per §512, to remove any potentially infringing content by sending an email with the alleged infringement with all pertinent requirements to a dedicated email address.

Governing Law

On the off chance you are sued, you want to make sure you aren't hauled into court in some remote jurisdiction of your user, but rather a court you are familiar with, preferably where your company transacts its business. Some websites are silent on governing law, but you should always try to get the more favorable jurisdiction for your company. The Governing Law provision should be drafted to give your company home-court advantage (no pun intended).

Arbitration Clause

Although it's not something that is required, I am a big fan of arbitration language in legal agreements, which your terms of use are. Many large companies refrain from including arbitration in a contract, as it is to their benefit to draw out proceedings for as long as possible and run up legal bills—a well-known tactic to force the little guy into settlement or, better yet, give up because he can't afford to fight the court battle. Arbitration clauses, however, are more expeditious. They are usually presided over by former practitioners or judges, and are more streamlined, making it an easier process for consumers. An added benefit is that arbitrations are private grievance forums, unlike court proceedings, which are public records.

Because binding arbitration language is drafted in a way that requires participants to give up their constitutional right to have their grievances heard by a court of law, it is imperative that your arbitration clause highlight and acknowledge this fact. That is why you will find most arbitration language in bold print, capitalized, or otherwise drafted to be "in your face." This bolding, underscoring, or emphasis doesn't give this or any other highlighted language in an agreement any more validity than language in regular type, but it certainly stands out from the rest of the agreement. If people read nothing else, they tend to at least read (or skim) emphasized terms.

WEBSITE CONTENT AND MARKETING MATERIALS

Marketing materials are often not given too much thought from a legal perspective. It bears mentioning, especially since this is a book about the legalities of small businesses and entrepreneurs, that you may not use copyrighted material in your marketing materials. I can hear you now, *"Of course! I would never plagiarize!"* (Insert eyeroll.) But words strung together aren't the only things that are copyrighted and protected. Photos and images are copyrighted material and using them without permission can land you in big trouble.

Practically speaking, this means you can't pull a picture off of the internet and use it on your homepage, in your newsletter or marketing materials—not a picture of a flower, a city skyline or a celebrity. If it is on the internet, that image is protected by copyright. As you will learn in the copyright chapter later, just by taking the picture, you are deemed the legal owner and have a common law copyright in the photograph. Whomever took that photo and put it up on the internet has, at the very least, a copyright that is protected by common law, so be careful reposting other people's pictures. If the owner has taken the steps to perfect the registration with the copyright office, then you may find yourself staring down the barrel of huge statutory fees for copyright infringement. Tread lightly. I have had several people file into my office over the years, not understanding why they are getting served with very aggressive and expensive copyright infringement letters from someone's attorney. This is an instance where it is easier to ask for permission than forgiveness.

If you are looking to use images up on your site that are not yours, there are plenty of free libraries out there. Simply google "stock images" or "free images" and you will be given a host of alternatives to choose from. Some sites, such as Pexels and Stock Photo Secrets, are completely free, and you may even use the photos for commercial purposes without attribution (credit) or payment. However, when searching for these free photos, you will undoubtedly come across sites that tout "royalty-free images." Understand that there's a big difference in *free images* and *royalty-free* images. Free is completely free, no payment to the site or copyright holder whatsoever. Royalty-free means that you pay a fee to the site to license the use of the photo, but you are free from paying royalties to the copyright holder each time you're using the photo, nor do you have to account for any royalty payments in the event that the use of the photo generates a profit.

It is important to note that many of these free and royalty-free sites do not contain celebrity images. If you are a blogger, or if you post pop-culture content and want to *gag* over how Beyoncé dropped another album at midnight, you are not going to find any celebrity images on the free sites to accompany that blog post. You can't just go and take an image from another website and put that on your blog or in your newsletter. Misappropriation of celebrity images is what trips a lot of people up and results in hefty fines. The paparazzi own and license their photos for profit. Trust and believe they didn't hide behind bushes and jump in front of cars only to have that image co-opted by a blogger who wants to dish the latest dirt. If you're looking for a celebrity image, head over to Shutterstock,

Adobe or Getty. You will pay a fee to license the photo for a specific time. But know that it is substantially less than paying lawyer's fees and the resultant damages incurred for copyright infringement. A website's legalities is part of the business that is often overlooked, but by putting just a little time and effort into it, the right website will save you a lot of time and expense in the long run.

Don't Get in Over Your Head

> *"We must learn our limits. We are all something, but none of us are everything."*
>
> — Blaise Pascal

THIS IS A GOOD ONE. If lawyers could speak freely, I would have so much tea to spill on cleaning up behind people. Whether it's someone trying a DIY on a project they should just P-A-Y someone to do, such as trademarking (more on that next), or the other way around: a contractor/business taking on a job they are not qualified to do. One word: *don't*. Don't do it. I see this so much in my profession. This is one of the most crucial nuggets of wisdom I routinely share.

Doing something you're unqualified to do, whether for yourself or a client, is a huge mistake. And it is a temptation that almost every entrepreneur will encounter. As an early-stage business owner having invested a lot of your capital, or if business is slow, be particularly mindful of the temptation to take on something that is not in your wheelhouse. If you've never handled that type of project or transaction, please don't start now, as you're enrolling in the school of hard knocks. And this steep learning curve will invariably be at another's (or your) expense. As a mentor told me years ago, "All money ain't good money," and in this instance, it can lead to financial repercussions and damage to your reputation or your own business. If you're a business owner, it's just not ethical to play with someone's livelihood on your learning curve! And if you're doing a DYI on your own business, the results can be disastrous.

There are ways to make this a win-win for you and your client. If you want to learn about a particular industry or business and not completely turn over your opportunity to someone else, find a seasoned professional and ask if you can shadow them. Shadowing is one of the best ways to learn the business; in fact, I earned my first $500 in the film industry by shadowing a seasoned entertainment lawyer. I had a theoretical knowledge of the industry and someone brought me a lucrative opportunity I was not prepared for. The potential client needed this agreement done quickly, so with the client's permission, I referred him to a more seasoned entertainment attorney, Darren. I shadowed Darren on the matter and had several Q&A sessions with him learning the ins and outs of this particular type of industry agreement. Because of ethical reasons, attorneys can't pay referral fees, and I couldn't justify a fee split as I wasn't "working" on the deal. I was learning. But I gained intellectual currency. I learned! In turn, Darren later paid me $500 to review and mark up another one of his client's agreements. This was a lot of money back then, but heck, it could have paid five dollars and I would have done it. That was my first "real" film agreement and my first paycheck in the film industry, so it was a win-win. Don't ever underestimate the value of intellectual currency and learning under another professional. Your time will come, and when it does, you will be ready.

Conversely, if you are early in your business and trying to cut corners or save money on attorney's fees, this is the area where you may want to try to reorganize your resources. Although what attorneys do may look easy, it's not. There is a reason we went to law school and invested a great amount of time and resources to learn our craft. Although I love music, and have watched my clients work for years, I don't think for a second that I can produce a beat, yet alone one that will be a success. I can write articles and I wrote this book, but I highly doubt that I can write a successful screenplay off the flip. People's work is a craft that they have spent years perfecting, and to think you can do it just as easily or successfully is often a tale of fool's gold.

If you've taken time to write your business plan, you will know the resources that you need. I often tell people that you can build a house on a foundation of mud, and if you are not properly allocating money for the basic resources to make your business successful, you can't expect it to be a success. People freely pay money for PR and marketing but come to a lawyer after the fact, with little to no money, trying to bargain us down because they are a "small business" with limited resources. Here's some TEA: you need your legalities in order *before* you even start to market your business. If you haven't applied for or secured your trademark, you shouldn't even be marketing your business; if you haven't properly formed your corporate entity, your taxes could be a disaster, which can devastate your business. Properly set aside some money to pay for the resources you need to get your business across the finish line and remember the old adage: it takes money to make money.

Chapter 7

TRADEMARKS

"They didn't trademark everything back then.
Now someone farts and they put a ™ *after it!"*

— Michael Jackson

CONSIDERING this is a book for entrepreneurs, I would be remiss if I didn't focus on your intellectual property. After all, this is your business and what you are creating is *your* idea. Intellectual property (IP) is just that: something you created. IP covers literary and artistic works, designs, inventions, graphics, and names—including your company's name, your products' names and, in certain instances, your government name or moniker. You will often hear people say that you need to protect your IP. But what does that mean? It means you are afforded the exclusive right to use the IP in a certain category while excluding others from making, using and selling the protected IP under the same name or design in that category. By default, some IP is afforded certain common law protections once used in commerce or reduced to a tangible mode of expression, such as putting it down on paper. But common law only affords certain rights— and we are savvy entrepreneurs—so I am giving you the TEA on how to legally protect what you have created.

The World Intellectual Property Organization ("WIPO") classifies IP into six categories: trademark, copyright, patent, trade secrets, industrial designs and geographical indications. Your protection is based on what category your IP falls under. For example, trademark registration protects words, symbols, phrases, slogans, logos (what we will refer to as "mark(s)" in this chapter). A patent protects designs, inventions and processes. You seek federal registration and protection for trademarks and patents from the United States Patent and Trademark Office ("USPTO"). Copyrights protect works of authorship, sound recordings, scripts, treatments, photos, animated images, maps and the like. For this, you seek federal registration through the United States Copyright Office. Federal registration means you have broader geographical and enforcement rights for your IP and allows for statutory damages in the case of infringement.

Trademarks used in connection with services, as opposed to products, are referred to as "servicemarks." Both trademarks and servicemarks are proprietary rights that give the owner exclusive protection and prevent others from using that name in that same class of service. The idea is, you want to prevent the likelihood of confusion in the mind of the consumer and identify the goods and services as yours.

In the United States, Canada and a few other jurisdictions, you obtain what is called a "common law" right (which is different from a registered trademark) when your marks are used in connection with goods or services even *before* you register it with the USPTO. Common law ownership lasts as long as there is a continual use of the mark in commerce *in that geographical area*. It is evidenced by the use of the "™" behind the name. But beware: common law trademarks do not have federal protection. They are based in state law, thus the protection extends only to a certain geographical region (i.e., the state where you use that mark), and the owner may only obtain limited damages in the event of an infringement.

By obtaining federal registration of your mark with the USPTO, the mark is listed in the federal database, which puts others on notice that you are the owner of that mark nationwide—not just in that particular state. Other benefits of federal registration include having the ability to sue for damages to recover lost profits; being able to receive statutory damages (remedies available by law) in the case of an infringement, such as triple (e.g., treble) damages for a willful infringement of the mark; and recovering attorney's fees and costs in the event you prevail in your infringement claim.

You may be wondering whether you can apply for a worldwide trademark. Trademarks are federal, and specific to the United States. However, if you have a trademark application pending before the USPTO, you may seek registration in any of the 122 countries (as of this book's publication date) that are members of the Madrid Protocol by filing an "international application" with WIPO through the USPTO. You may register your trademark in other countries during or after you become the registered owner of a federal trademark.

The mistake many entrepreneurs make is branding themselves with a catchy name/slogan before searching the mark to see if it's already being used in commerce, meaning the mark is already subject to a common law protection or federal trademark registration. If you use the same name as another entity in that same class of service subsequent to their common law or registered trademark, you are committing trademark infringement. There are databases and watch organizations that help owners police their marks, so most likely the infringement will come to light sooner rather than later. As mentioned, if the mark is a registered trademark, you will be facing actual and treble damages, and those damages quickly add up. So, let's get started to make sure you properly handle your trademark registration.

I recommend hiring a trademark attorney as you begin your quest. When you schedule your consultation with the attorney, be clear on the name and how you intend to use it. This is important, because the USPTO divides trademarks into 45 different "classes" which identify how your potential mark will be used. Classes one to 34 are for "goods"; 35 to 45 are reserved for "services." You need to be class specific, as you can't *just* trademark a name. Again, trademarks are meant to avoid the likelihood of confusion *in a particular class.* A list of Trademark Classes is found in Appendix B.

Think of the product Dove, for example. "Which one?" you may ask. Exactly. There are at least two household-named products for sale on the market under the trade name Dove. There are Dove soap products owned by Unilever and registered in Class 3 (which covers bleaching preparations and other substances for laundry use; cleaning, polishing, scouring and abrasive preparations; soaps; perfumery, essential oils, cosmetics, hair lotions; and dentifrices). Dove Chocolates, owned by Mars on the other hand, is registered in Class 30 (which covers coffee, tea, cocoa, sugar, rice, tapioca, sago, artificial coffee; flour and preparations made from cereals, bread, pastry and confectionery, ices; honey, treacle; yeast, baking powder; salt, mustard; vinegar, sauces (condiments); spices; and ice). Same with Delta. There's Delta Airlines and Delta Faucets. The two products are registered in two distinct classes, Delta Airlines covering transportation services, while Delta Faucets' trademark covers goods, specifically relating to plumbing and faucets The products can co-exist because they are registered in two different classes, therefore avoiding the likelihood of confusion in that particular class.

In some instances, you may want to register your good or service in multiple classes. Let's say you're a band. You'll register your band name in Class 41, which covers education; providing of training; entertainment; sporting and cultural activities. If you want to sell T-shirts and hoodies, you may also want to register in Class 25, which covers clothing, footwear and headgear. But merchandise isn't a "class," so if you also want to sell the group's backpacks or gym bags, that would require registration in a different class, Class 18, which covers leather and imitations of leather, and goods made of these materials and not included in other classes; animal skins, hides; trunks and traveling bags; umbrellas, parasols and walking sticks; whips, harnesses and saddlery. Now you understand why you have to have a crystal-clear idea of exactly how you want to use your goods or services before heading down the trademark road.

Your attorney may want to perform a trademark search in order to discover whether the name is already being used. To do this, the attorney hires a third-party company to perform a comprehensive search of all federal, state and common law databases, as well phone directories, business directories, websites, social media sites and any pending applications in the USPTO. The attorney should then issue an opinion letter outlining the current marks and potential conflicts that may prevent you from obtaining a federal registration with the USPTO. It also satisfies any due diligence issues that may arise at a later date, in case you are faced with a claim of trademark infringement.

Two very important things to remember with a search: First, a trademark search is comprehensive and expensive; therefore many people choose to proceed without it. Do this at your own risk. If you can't afford for an attorney to perform a search and offer the opinion letter, at least try to perform one on your own by searching the web and doing a deep dive. Begin with the USPTO and search in their TEAS database for any registered trademarks. Also search the state database. Remember: if you are not applying for federal trademark protection, you need only to check the state in which your mark will be used in commerce. If you are seeking federal registration, you will need to check every state's database. It's a good idea to do a comprehensive online search to cover as many bases as possible. In this instance, something is better than nothing before filing. Secondly, it is important to remember that these searches are only as current as the search itself and the pending registrations. Once you determine the mark is available, either register the mark immediately or begin using the mark as quickly as possible. Trademarking is definitely a race of first use *and* first to file when determining the presumption of ownership. If you are the first to use a trademark, but someone else was the first to register the name with the USPTO, you will have to get a trademark attorney involved to help resolve this issue. Having a registered trademark grants the owner protection as the presumptive legal owner of the name, placing the burden of proof on the one challenging the validity of the trademark.

Now that you have searched the mark and determined no other person or entity is using it, how do you file for federal trademark protection? As of October 2019, all trademark registrations must be filed electronically with the USPTO—snail mail applications are no longer accepted. There are two filing options: The TEAS Plus option, which has a filing fee of $250 per class but has more requirements up front. Most practitioners use the TEAS Standard filing option, which has fewer up-front requirements and runs $350 per class. Regardless, the fee is based on the number of classes you are registering, not the number of goods sought within that class, so you may register multiple goods in a class for the one flat fee. That is welcome news because trademarking is replete with fees, requirements and deadlines, so one less expense to worry about.

To begin your application, you have to declare a *filing basis.* There are four bases upon which you may file your application:

Intent to Use

Just as it sounds. An intent to use means you have not yet used your goods or services "in commerce," but you plan to do so in the foreseeable future. I recommend you file the ITU as soon as you have a good idea of what your goods or services will be. Think of the IU as a placeholder while you start to manufacture or sell your products or services.

Use in Commerce

Your intended mark is already in active use in interstate or international commerce in that particular class.

Foreign Registration Basis

You already own a foreign trademark registration in your country of origin for the *same* mark for the *same* goods and/or services.

Foreign Application Basis

You filed a foreign application within six months of your U.S. application for the same mark and the same goods and/or services.

Trademark applications are deceptively simple, which is why most laypeople try to file the trademark themselves. But as the saying goes: *The devil is in the details.* And the devil seems to be running all up and through the trademark application. The application requires you to set forth, in specificity, a description of the goods or services you are using in commerce. This is the point where most people who self-file or use a filing service such as LegalZoom have issues, and the application is rejected. Why? Well, the descriptions must be narrowly tailored and accurate; the use of "descriptive" words or phrases will be rejected. The application can also be rejected based on the "likelihood of confusion" and a few other reasons, as the application's wording is akin to an art form best left in the hands of a professional.

As aforementioned, in order to register the trademark, you have to prove that you are actually using your mark in commerce. To that end, you must provide acceptable proof or *specimens* of every product or service you are seeking to register; you are showing the trademark office that you are actually selling these goods, not simply advertising. The specimens of use are determined by category and class. Acceptable specimens of products include:

- Websites or catalogues which show that the product is available for sale
- Point-of-sale advertising (hang tags, labels, etc.)
- Packaging materials

Unacceptable product specimens include:
- Media or PR releases announcing your product is for sale
- Business cards
- Price list
- Brochures

Acceptable specimens for services include:
- Billboards
- Newspaper, magazine or digital advertisements (including social media pages)
- Menus
- Letterhead, invoices or other business documents, provided that they contain the mark and outline the services

Unacceptable service specimens include:
- Media or PR releases announcing your services
- Articles that mention your services

Once you have successfully submitted your application and the examiner has accepted the application and specimens, assuming there aren't any issues with the filing, the office will issue a notice of publication. This notification may take up to six or nine months, so don't be alarmed during prolonged periods of silence from the USPTO. The trademark office will publish the name, which then puts the public on notice that you are seeking to register the trademark and gives the public a chance to object based on the "likelihood of confusion." If the waiting period elapses without any objection, you are issued a trademark registration, evidenced by a certificate—the ® symbol vs. the "™" symbol (which only applies to common law uses of a trademark). If your application is refused, the examiner will issue an "Office Action" outlining the issues associated with your application. You have six months to fix the issue before the USPTO grants a refusal. There are several reasons why you may get an Office Action, but the most common reasons are substantive issues such as the "likelihood of confusion," citing the mark as "descriptive," or technical deficiencies, such as the need for disclaimers, improper specimens, and insufficient or improper identification of your goods or services. This is the moment at which, if you haven't consulted a trademark attorney, you should, so they can properly defend your application. Trying to fix a botched trademark application is far more difficult and costly than hiring a trademark attorney from the beginning. The odds are also not in your favor, and depending how badly you've boxed yourself in, your efforts may be DOA, requiring you to start over, which is costly and extremely frustrating.

In the event you have successfully obtained registration of your mark, the work doesn't end there. Every five years, you must file "Declarations" with the USPTO to demonstrate you are using the mark in commerce or your mark could expire. Every 10 years, you must also file to renew your trademark. In both instances, you are required to submit the Specimens of Use to the USPTO as evidencing your continued use.

Congratulations! You are now the owner of a registered trademark, and just like anything else that you own, you are responsible for it. In trademark-speak, that means you have to protect and defend the mark against any potential infringers—those who are using the same name or a similar name in a category that is likely to cause confusion in the mind of the consumer. Because there are no shortage of names or new ideas in this country of 330 million people, unless you're stringing together some unheard-of name, someone at some point is likely to try to use your name, slogan or mark in your category of business. The more common the mark, the more potential infringers. Keeping an eye on your mark becomes a herculean task, so you may want to hire a monitoring service that tracks and alerts you of potential problems. If you cannot hire a firm, consider investing in monitoring software that will at the very least notify you of potential issues.

In the event that someone does infringe on your mark, you have the right to sue to protect your mark. Registered trademarks are afforded statutory remedies and damages in the event of a trademark infringement, while common law trademarks are not afforded the same. The Lanham Act is murky on how courts actually award recovery, but pursuant to the Act, a trademark owner may seek to recover monetary damages in the event of the following: 1) disgorgement of the defendant's profits; 2) actual damages, 3) reasonable royalties otherwise due, 4) attorney's fees in exceptional cases and 5) costs. In some instances of blatant and egregious infringements, the courts award a plaintiff treble damages, a punitive move by the courts that provides that the infringer pay you three times the actual damages as a punitive move by the courts for bold and outrageous behavior.

Bottom line, a federal trademark registration offers the most protection for your mark. Start early with an online search of your own prior to branding yourself and hire a proficient trademark attorney to assist you in your endeavors. This, like other areas of the law, is where an ounce of prevention is worth a pound of cure, because if you go about the trademark apple incorrectly, you may not get a second bite.

APPENDIX B: TRADEMARK CLASS APPENDIX

The Importance of Networking

NETWORKING! Just the mention of the word gives me the creeps. Yes, it is necessary, but the way that it plays out just doesn't jibe right with me. It's often attending curated events with name tags, targeted socializing, asking or emailing professionals you meet to pick their brains. If I had a dollar (heck, even 25 cents) for every time that has happened, I could've purchased my dream beach house…which is on my vision board, btw!

Networking is an artform, but when not handled right, it comes across akin to social climbing that leaves everyone feeling empty with no connections. However, when handled properly, networking can yield tremendous results. Please don't underestimate the power of social currency and building meaningful relationships. Networking often results in finding a mentor, job introductions and business referrals. It's a powerful tool in any industry, and especially so for entrepreneurs. I have built my entire career through networking; I have *never* advertised my services. All of my corporate and individual clients have come about as a result of relationships I've built and nurtured over the years. I also get referrals from clients and other professionals that I know or have worked with/for; word of mouth, interpersonal and technical skills go a long way. In networking and establishing your business contacts, you must be organic yet strategic, kind and witty, yet not a know-it-all or obnoxious. And you have to approach the meetings and introductions correctly. First impressions are lasting impressions, and you don't get a second chance to make a first impression. People tend to hire and work with people who they like and those relationships are often formed at work events, conferences and tradeshows — networking events. The *way* you network and people's responses matter, so that's what I want to spill the tea on: creating those organic connections that yield meaningful relationships with *big* results.

Networking is like a dance, a tango if you will. There has to be a give and take. The most common mistake people make is not recognizing that this is a bilateral transaction. Executives and C-suite professionals are extremely busy, and honestly, we get an insane amount of emails asking for advice or to "pick our brains." 99.9 percent are from people whom I have *never* met, who've never laid eyes on me. Someone who randomly contacts me or reaches out after an event asking me to pour into them. That's a big ask, and the way it's mostly done is a big turn off! Remember, it's a dance, a give and take.

By all means, if you're trying to meet someone, the last resort should be the cold call. To me, that shows that you haven't made the effort to go out and form relationships on your own at networking events. There are a million associations, meetings, meet-ups, festivals and organizations that you could have attended and met me or that someone you're looking to meet, so just try. You have to be in it to win it, meaning you have to be in those rooms to make things (i.e., meetings and introductions) happen. So, get out (even virtually) and be in the "rooms" to form those personal networks.

LinkedIn is the world's largest professional networking portal, with over a half billion members in over 200 countries. You may connect with people in your educational, workplace or companies of interest digitally through the portal to establish and flesh out your networks. LinkedIn also has a host of groups and forums of like-minded industry professionals where you can take courses, participate in discussions and share your experience. Be interactive in these forums; speak up and engage in the conversations. To get started, curate and be intentional in setting up your professional profile. You'll want to highlight your education, organizations and accomplishments, as well as follow companies and organizations in your industry. Highlight your strengths, specializations, skills which allow others to endorse your professional services, skills which serve as digital advertising, and recommendations that other professionals on the site can draw from when looking at your profile.

People meet a lot of people at the average event, so your follow-up is where you can really stand out and set yourself apart from the crowd. For example, in your follow-up email, find that common ground, which will be the great equalizer. This common ground needn't be about the legal world—heck, if you've researched me or listened to me at that event, you'd know I have wanderlust. Include an article about some new travel gadget; a dope hotel in some far-flung destination; a healthy recipe you tried that was awesome as a follow-up to that non-business tidbit we discussed ("How did that Pad Thai recipe turn out?"). Something. Anything to set yourself apart and let me know that I am not just one of 100 people you met and are following up with to simply "pick my brain."

I find it helpful to make a note on the back of the business card (if they have a card, which is increasingly rare these days) or e-card you received. Write down that trivial bit you discussed, make notes and listen. Most people don't listen; we are so busy trying to formulate our question or comeback that we fail to actually listen in order to have a reciprocal conversation. (Note: Listening is also an artform that will serve you in every area of your personal and professional life, as well.)

In my Mentoring Tea Time later, I talk about my now friend, Carlton. Carlton wasn't in law school. He followed me on Twitter and introduced himself at a journalism conference I attended. When he came up to me, Carlton rattled off some trivial something about travel I'd tweeted and we organically fell into a conversation. Later, he offered to take *me* to lunch at his favorite Tex-Mex restaurant when I came back to Houston because he knew I loved Mexican food! I took him up on the lunch invitation because I loved his energy. Of course, I paid, but the offer was a classy move! Now that's how you make yourself stand out from the crowd.

On the other hand, let's say you know a person who knows the person you'd like to meet. Unless you have a very familiar relationship (mentor/mentee, close friend, etc.), employ those same tools when you reach out to ask for the introduction. Remember, your contact is probably just as busy as the person you're trying to meet, so approach that ask the way you would approach your intended executive. Again, realize that we get asked for a lot of introductions, so come prepared. But first, your email: please, *please* open it sincerely and with grace. Ask how they are doing, ask about their holidays, how they're holding up in the pandemic, etc. *Then* get down to business. Remember the dance: the give is showing that you are interested in their well-being, asking about them—not just bombarding them off the flip with your ask (the take). In your ask, be clear and succinct. Tell me why you want me to reach out for the introduction, and how you can be an asset to that person or their company. Send along your résumé or CV as an attachment, so I don't have to email you back and ask for that. Remember, time is money, so don't waste it.

If handled correctly, you are setting yourself up to win with networking. Remember, people tend to do business with people they like and are familiar with. So, organically, be in it to win it.

Chapter 8

COPYRIGHT

"Words are the only things that last forever."

— William Hazlitt

ONE OF THE most common questions I get is, "How do I copyright my idea?" The Constitution was written and this country was founded to foster an exchange of ideas to increase capitalism, so stymieing someone's creativity was not what our Founding Fathers intended.

Listen up: Ideas are not copyrightable, although the way in which they are expressed may be. Let me repeat that: you cannot copyright an *idea*, but you may seek to protect *how* you express that idea.

Let's use the example of Mark Burnett, who had the idea of a three-panel judge music competition show, *American Idol*. If Burnett was able to copyright his *idea* of a singing show where panelists perform in front of three judges, we would never have had *The Voice* or any of the other five or so musical competition shows that *Idol* spawned. So, although he wasn't able to protect the underlying show idea (singing show with three panel judges), he was able to copyright the script and format of the show. Therefore, any other three panel judge/singing show had to differentiate itself. Ergo, *The Voice* has blind auditions and their three judges sit in spinning chairs and have teams… Well, you get the point.

Now back to copyrights, and what that is exactly. A copyright is a form of protection grounded in the U.S. Constitution and granted by law for original works of authorship reduced to a tangible medium of expression. Copyright covers both published and unpublished works. Copyright protects original works of authorship (including, but not limited to, literary, dramatic, musical, and artistic such as poetry, novels, movies, songs, computer software and architecture) from the moment the work is reduced to a tangible mode of expression (i.e., written down). Prior to 1978, you had to re-register your work upon publication. Fortunately, that is no longer the case. Once you have a copyright, it is secured for the life of the author plus 70 years.

Although copyright and trademark both provide protection, copyright differs from trademark. To put it simply, copyrights protect original works of authorship (a script, book, song, treatment). A trademark, as we learned, protects words, phrases, symbols or designs identifying the goods or services and distinguishing them from the ideas of others. (Patents protect designs and inventions, but patents are a highly specialized area of law, and are too technical for this primer. Considering you must use a lawyer to file a patent, we'll leave that discussion to you and your patent attorney.)

Just as you are afforded certain common law trademark protection without formally filing your mark (by being first to use a name, slogan, etc.—see chapter 7), you are afforded copyright protection without formally registering your work with the copyright office. Meaning, as soon as you have reduced your idea to a tangible mode of expression (writing, typing, recording), you have a copyright. I'm sure you've heard of the "poor man's copyright," whereby you mail yourself a poem and have a copyright? You don't even have to do that to have a common law copyright. Even if you wrote your poem in your journal, you have a copyright, and you can put the copyright symbol © on that work.

But just as you obtain federal benefits and protections by registering your trademark with the USPTO, the same holds true for copyrights. And the good news is, it's not difficult. Unlike the trickery and sorcery of filing a trademark application, registering a copyright is very simple. It's so simple that the benefits of taking 30 minutes to register your works far outweigh any reasons for not registering. If you register your work, you will be afforded certain protections:

- You can sue in federal court.
- You can seek statutory damages (more on this below) in your lawsuit if you registered any time before the potential infringement or if you obtained a copyright three months prior to publication of your work. If you don't have a registered copyright, you can only sue for actual damages.
- If you obtain a copyright within five years after the first date of publication, what is contained in the copyright certificate is deemed correct, thus the burden shifts to the defendant to disprove they did not commit copyright infringement.
- You have a public record of ownership that declares you as the rightful owner.
- It allows for an assignment of rights. In the case of music, scripts or anything you might actually assign to a third party, the third party will most likely want proof of registration to avoid a chain of title problems down the line.

So, what about those statutory damages? According to 17 USC subsection 504 (b), if someone infringes on your copyright, you have the ability to sue and collect on the amount of your "actual" damages and any profits the infringer has collected. If you timely filed your copyright, you can elect statutory damages, which provides anywhere from $750 to $30,000 per work that was infringed, and that number increases up to $150,000 for each copyright infringement of the work if the judge finds the infringement was willful.

Absent copyright registration, you don't have the ability to collect attorney's fees and costs. Per the rules of law in the U.S., the agreement to collect and pay attorney's fees and costs must be agreed upon by both parties in writing. This agreement usually comes in the form of a contract that has an "Indemnification" section which includes a provision along the lines of: *The prevailing party shall be entitled to collect any attorney's fees and costs in connection with the enforcement of this Agreement.*

In the case of copyright infringement, there is no written agreement for the use of the work, so there is nowhere for the parties to agree to attorney's fees and costs. However, Section 7 USC 412 grants the copyright holder reimbursement of attorney's fees and court costs associated with the infringement in the event you prevail in your case. The attorney's fees provision coupled with a registration may make a suit palatable for a lawyer to take on, even if you don't have the money to hire an attorney up front, as the lawyer has the ability to collect a rather large sum on the backend. This is what is known as Contingency Fee representation.

If you have an unregistered work, you are limited to actual damages (meaning what you actually lost, and good luck proving that), so simply bringing your case to trial might not make dollars and sense because of the small amount of potential recovery. Black out your fees for paying the attorney to represent you, and you may be at a wash.

To apply for a copyright, simply visit the official copyright office at copyright.gov and browse the FAQs to familiarize yourself with the process and different forms available for various works. Complete the application, upload your work, and pay $35 per work submitted. If you mail in your application and work, the application fee increases to $65 and your registration is delayed by months. If you are submitting multiple works (a "collection of works" to use copyright office verbiage), you may register them all at once, provided you are the author of all of the works, and further, provided said works were published together at the same time. The best example of this is a recording artist who releases an album or an author who publishes an anthology of stories. If your copyright application is successful, the copyright office will send you a certificate and registration is retroactive to the date the copyright office received all your materials to complete your application. Remember that unlike a trademark, it's simple to do, there is no maintenance, and your works are now afforded copyright protection for the life of the author (you) plus 70 years!

When you are an entrepreneur, you want to make sure you are protecting your IP, whether you are a freelancer or if you are a small business owner. You may think that you don't have any IP to protect; after all, you're not writing any books or screenplays. But employee work product has long been the status subject of countless litigation. Although it is widely held in most states that a work product created by an employee is property of the employer, it is incumbent on the employer to prove such works were created while the employee was actually employed, or that the employee's creation is otherwise subject to ownership per the employment agreement.

Let me give you a $500,000,000 example.

There is a very famous lawsuit, *Mattel v. Bryant*, that underscores this concept. Carter Bryant was employed by Mattel designing clothes for Mattel's famous Barbie doll line. While Bryant was on a seven-month hiatus from Mattel, he began designing another line of dolls and put together a prototype from various pieces of old clothes and toys around his house. The dolls were meant to be a line of design-your-own, pick-your-skin-tone dolls created for "bratty, clothes obsessed teens, with diverse backgrounds." Shortly before Bryant resigned from Mattel in 2001, he sold this prototype design (his IP) to MGA Entertainment. This prototype was what eventually became the Bratz Dolls. By the end of that year, MGA had sold nearly $97 million worth of Bratz Dolls; two years later, that number had jumped to one billion dollars in sales by 2003. By 2004, a mere three years after Bryant's sale of his Bratz to MGA, sales had reached nearly $2 billion. Bryant was now a super-rich man, raking in a whopping $35 million in revenue in sales and royalties from his deal with MGA.

At that point, however, the Bratz Dolls' uber popularity was cutting into Mattel's market share, threatening to knock Barbie off her sales pedestal. Mattel would have none of that. After all, Barbie had dominated doll sales since its inception in 1959. So, later that year, Mattel sued Bryant, citing copyright infringement among other claims seeking restitution for that $35 million in sales and royalties. Mattel's argument was that Bryant's employment contract assigned all of his "inventions" during his employment to Mattel. This is a standard and customary clause in many employment agreements. The company is paying for your work product, so ostensibly, everything you create while under the company's employ is assigned to your employer. Since Bryant was employed by Mattel when he conceived and worked on the Bratz prototype, the intellectual property to the dolls belonged to Mattel, who demanded all $30 million of Bryant's profits. After nearly six years of suits, countersuits and appeals, Bryant and Mattel ultimately settled out of court in an undisclosed settlement and hundreds of thousands of dollars in lawyer's fees.

The (very expensive) lesson here is that most employers, under the law, own your intellectual property. If you are employing full time, part-time, term or "at-will" workers (meaning the employee can be terminated for any reason, or no reason at all, at any time), all employers should provide an offer letter in writing to underscore that the IP belongs to the company. In addition to the terms of employment, the offer letter to the employee should outline that all of the "results and proceeds of employees work are a work for hire pursuant to Section 17 USC subsection 101, specially ordered and commissioned by employer." Look at it this way: your money, your time. You own it.

Similarly, you should give any consultants you hire a "Work for Hire" agreement which outlines the same: any ideas or work product created is your product, not theirs. This includes web designers, graphic artists, anyone working on your project. A properly worded consultant agreement transfers the copyright to the employer. Conversely, if you are an employee or consultant and happen to be writing a book, for example, prior to your employment and continue working on the book, you should try to exempt your intellectual property from the company.

Registering your copyright and using the appropriate paperwork will protect you in the long and short term. It is inexpensive, quick and easy, leaving no excuse not to do it. And in this instance, an ounce of prevention is worth a pound of cure.

APPENDIX C: WORK FOR HIRE AGREEMENT

The Importance of Mentoring

"After the verb 'to love,' 'to help'
is the most beautiful verb in the world."

— Bertha von Suttner

THE NOTION OF mentoring came from Greek mythology, in Homer's *The Odyssey*. When Odysseus, king of Ithaca, left this kingdom to fight in the Trojan War, he entrusted its care to Mentor—who not only oversaw the kingdom, but also served as the teacher and overseer of Odysseus' son, Telemachus. And the rest, as we say, is history.

Mentoring continues today and is instrumental in the professional development of our future leaders. A mentor is a professional role model who guides the mentee's growth and development over a period of time. A mentor shares knowledge and wisdom, draws out the possibilities and helps to provide a roadmap on how to get where you are going.

Mentoring is a way that I have given back in the legal profession and has given me an enormous sense of pride and accomplishment. When I started out as a young lawyer, especially a Black female attorney in a white man's industry, I didn't have a lot of mentors, as there just weren't a lot of women in this area.

But fortunately, I did have people who believed in me, my smarts and my hustle.

Keenan Ivory Wayans was the first one to reach out and help me, and for that, I am forever grateful. I met Keenan through his wife, Daphne, and I spent countless hours at their house. They were truly my second family when I moved to Los Angeles as a young lawyer. At the time, Keenan was a very in-demand screenwriter and actor, and still executive producing *In Living Color*. But he recognized what I was doing to teach myself entertainment law (and we were often talking "business"), Keenan offered to introduce me to his entertainment lawyer, Stephen Barnes, and set up a call with him. When I called Stephen, he immediately offered to meet with me because Keenan had never asked him to meet with anyone as a mentor, and therefore, Stephen knew I was serious about my business.

Stephen became my mentor. He regularly took me to lunch, and I always came prepared with questions as he helped guide and foster certain aspects of my career. Twenty plus years later, I choose Stephen as *my* entertainment lawyer when I have deals where I personally serve as talent, and now, my firm, Bonner Law PC, serves as outside counsel to his same firm, where I first sauntered into his office as a young lawyer, with a host of questions and a notebook, some 20-plus years earlier. Talk about a full-circle moment.

If you look back over your professional development, more than likely you had a mentor at some point, even if you didn't realize it at the time. Was there someone in your profession or someone in your office who you have had regular meals or conversations with, where you talked about your professional goals and objectives? Have you sought out that person's advice, "picked that person's brain" about your potential next professional move? Has that person shared the insight, offered suggestions? Well, you have had a mentor!

Similarly, when you are starting or expanding your business, you are at times going to need to turn to someone for advice and guidance. By mentoring someone, just think of that as paying good karma forward, because those tables will always turn, and you'll be the one looking for guidance at some point.

Speaking of those tables that always turn, just as Stephen was my mentor, when I became seasoned enough in my field to dispense information, I became a mentor. In fact, in 2007, after practicing for 10 years, I cofounded Black Women in Entertainment Law (BWEL) with 10 other female entertainment lawyers. We initially funded the organization from our own pockets, and we realized we were onto something and formally set up a nonprofit. In that capacity, I served as Executive Director for eight years. We were able to seek corporate funding and grants, and mentored aspiring BIPOC entertainment lawyers. We also organized and sponsored panels, professional networking events and speaking engagements, awarding over $450,000 in scholarship money during that time. Currently, I serve on the mentoring committee of the International Women's Forum, regularly meeting with young lawyers to give them guidance and serve as a resource for young and aspiring lawyers.

Karma never forgets an address, and my good fortune from serving as a mentor helped me launch my career as a travel influencer. I was at the National Association of Black Journalists convention in 2010 when a young man named Carlton chased me down. He was an aspiring journalist, so we met for coffee during the conference and stayed in touch. Fast forward a few months later, I'd tweeted that I was lecturing at a legal conference in Houston. Carlton inboxed me and asked if he could take *me* to lunch, which is a classy move. I accepted (and of course, I paid for lunch, but the offer was not lost on me), and Carlton mentioned he was interested in moving to New York City. I put him in touch with an editor of a magazine that I was providing counsel for and recommended him for the job. (Now, Carlton is sharp, so he landed that job on his own merits.) Here's where it gets interesting: because of Carlton's new job, he had access to a lot of information and resources that I wouldn't have known about; one of them being travel "influencers." In this nascent time of travel writing/influencers (they weren't called influencers until years later), things were very different, and these resources weren't readily available. Carlton was aware that I was writing travel pieces for various magazines and recommended that I sign up with this particular agency. Soon after signing up, I was contacted by a tourism board and took my first of many sponsored trips traveling and writing for travel publications, which I continued up until Covid, when all press trips were halted. Perfect example of how the teacher becomes the student, and how mentoring someone can lead to them teaching you about new things.

If you think about the invaluable relationship and the wisdom imparted to you and how that advice has helped shape your success, you understand the importance of doing the same for others. You don't have to establish your own mentoring organization like we did, nor do you have to formally join a mentoring organization to make a difference in a person's life. Regularly keeping in touch with someone by simply catching up for meals or coffee can make a world of difference in a person's professional development.

Mentoring is not to be confused with coaching or even sponsors. People generally hire a professional coach to help sort through professional and personal obstacles in their careers to achieve a specific goal or purpose. One seeks a coach for clarity, perspective and direction. You hire a coach to work with you for a set period of time, to identify and offer corrective techniques and instruction and perfect any issues that may be holding you back. The goal is to emerge with a fresh perspective and a roadmap for your next professional move.

Sponsors, on the other hand, are those who see that spark and potential in you and push you towards your next professional endeavor. A sponsor will stick her neck out for you by having conversations with other people about you, advocating for your advancement with the decision makers and positioning you to win! A sponsor isn't someone you pay; alternatively, this is someone who sees your potential and gratuitously puts their reputation on the line for you to advance in your career.

Sponsors are particularly important for women and BIPOC as we have been traditionally underrepresented in managerial levels and the C-suite. It bears mentioning that your sponsor doesn't have to match your race or gender; that is not important. What is important is developing an organic relationship with someone senior in your field who sees you, believes in you and can propel you. That, my dear, is a recipe for success.

Chapter 9

INSURANCE FOR YOUR SMALL BUSINESS

"By failing to prepare, you are preparing to fail."

— Benjamin Franklin

MANY PEOPLE are surprised when I ask if they've purchased insurance for their business. Just as you have insurance to protect your life, home and car, insuring your business investment is always a good idea. Your business may be affected by the death of a partner, an act of God, lawsuits, the injury of an employee or patron on your premises. As outlined in Chapter 3, if you have formed an LLC or a corporation, your personal assets should be protected from any liabilities of the business. But that doesn't address the other issues that can wreak financial havoc and potentially bankrupt your company. It's best to purchase insurance before you need it, because once you have a calamity, your business is considered high-risk. Your options then become limited and those that *are* available get very pricey.

Each state will have a different requirement for what type of insurance is required for your business, but let's break down the most common types of insurance for your business one by one.

Worker's Compensation Insurance: If you have employees, you are required by law to have worker's compensation insurance. Worker's compensation insurance provides for the payment of medical bills and wage replacement in the event an employee is injured on the job. The underlying premise is that an employer should provide a safe working environment, and if an employee is injured on the job during the normal course of employment, said employee should be able to receive compensation without having to prove fault or negligence of the employer. The employer's worker's compensation policy provides the insurance payments to the injured worker in exchange for his or her covenant not to sue the employer. The payments are intended to compensate the employee for lost wages while injured and to help fund the worker's medical bills. It is important to underscore that the worker is receiving insurance payments in exchange for giving up the right to sue and payments are generally based on actual damages; the calculation of punitive damages or pain and suffering are not considered in the amount that is calculated in determining the payout under worker's compensation. If the worker is killed during the course of employment, worker's compensation also pays future economic loss to the family.

Unemployment Insurance: Unemployment insurance is a state fund that employers pay into during the course of paying payroll taxes. It provides an insurance benefit, usually in the form of a weekly payout to the former worker, who collects funds directly from the state. Laws vary from state to state regarding the amount and length of payouts, but these payments generally come with stipulations that the employee was employed for some minimum amount of time and was terminated due to no fault of her own.

Disability insurance: Certain states—currently California, Hawaii, New York, New Jersey and Puerto Rico—have statutory disability programs, where the employee pays into the fund and may collect upon injury, but these state-funded payments only provide for short-term disability. The amount payable is calculated as a percentage of the worker's wages for the past 12 months.

Disability insurance, on the other hand, provides partial wage replacement to the worker in the event of a *non-work*-related accident. It's commonly referred to as "long-term disability insurance," because this insurance can be payable for up to the worker's lifetime. Although disability insurance is not required in every jurisdiction, carrying this type of insurance isn't a bad idea, as statistics report that one out of four Americans will suffer a disability before retirement.

Even if you are not employing any workers, you may want to take out disability insurance on yourself, because as a freelancer or entrepreneur, if you don't work, you don't get paid. Coverage and premiums vary depending on occupation, state of residence, insurance company and specific policy, so don't be deterred at the first quote. Shop around, because affordable insurance is out there; you just have to look for it and be willing to work within the parameters. Remember that disability insurance is not designed to cover 100% of your income. Insurers want you to get back to work, and typical policies pay out 40-80% of your income depending on the premiums you are willing to pay.

Other factors to keep in mind when you are shopping for disability coverage include your definition of "disability." The broader the definition of what constitutes a disability, the higher the premium; conversely, narrowing the definition of disability will result in lower premiums. Another thing to consider if you are financially able is taking out a policy with a longer waiting period before the reimbursement payments kick in, to obtain a lower premium. Lastly, if your budget allows, purchase a non-cancelable policy. Of course, your premiums will be higher, but your benefits will be locked in, and the insurance company doesn't have the option to cancel.

Professional Liability Insurance. If you are a lawyer, medical or dental provider, or other professional, your field (and in some instances, the state) may require you to obtain Professional Liability insurance, otherwise known as malpractice or Errors and Omissions insurance. A professional liability policy protects the professional from claims of malpractice and negligence from the very people they were intending to help. For instance, if a client didn't get the result they wanted, they may blame you; if the patient feels their physician botched the operation, the patient may be out for (your) blood. Liability insurance provides protection against claims of negligence, misrepresentation, malpractice and other missteps and errors specific to your field. Liability claims are very expensive to defend, and the cost to defend yourself could effectively wipe out your business. Moreover, if the plaintiff's claim is successful, the judgment could ostensibly bankrupt your business and perhaps you personally. Take precautions and obtain a professional liability policy if it is available for your profession.

Keyperson Insurance. This policy is a bit different policy as it doesn't cover goods and services of the business, but rather is a life insurance policy that is taken out on the life of a founder, top executive or a crucial member of your team. The insurance pays out on the death or disability of the crucial or "key" team member. This could be the founder, the head of research and development, the tech guru in your company or a key sales person, but if you want to cover more than one person, you would need a separate policy for each. Think about it as life insurance for the "company" which is intended to defray costs and provide operating capital in the event of the death of that key person. Just as the life insurance policy on a spouse would pay the beneficiary a survival benefit upon death, the same holds true in this instance. The company is the named beneficiary on a key person policy, and the proceeds would inure to the benefit of the business.

The benefits from the key person policy can be used as operating expenses for the business, for the costs of recruiting and training a suitable replacement, or a buy-back benefit, where you buy back the decedent's share of the business. You can also borrow against the policy, which reduces the ultimate payout, but this option can be a crucial lifeline if you run into unexpected expenses. If you determine that the business can't sustain itself after the transition, you may also use the proceeds to retire the business, and wind ups its affairs. The policy may be used to pay severance, pay off debts and your investor pool. The proceeds, if handled properly, can be tax free, provided that you have the key person's consent and have filed a Form 8925 with Uncle Sam.

Key person insurance is often a funding requirement for venture capitalists and angel investors. In addition to the Sharks asking about the patent on a product pitched on Shark Tank, the Sharks often ask about Key Person insurance. They want to make sure that these small businesses can survive the untimely death of that person responsible for developing (and often pitching) that product. Often at the funding stage of the game, the company is lean, often just a few crucial company members and if one dies, that missing piece could bankrupt the company without that financial parachute.

Crisis Insurance. Lastly, this option is a little-known policy that may be available to your business as a standalone insurance policy or, in some professions, may be an added benefit available under your Errors and Omissions or liability policy. This insurance is intended to help mitigate the damage to your company's reputation from negative press resulting from an issue or crisis at your business. In today's insta-society, cancel culture and rush to disseminate information in nearly real time, the stakes are higher than ever to protect your company's reputation.

Crisis management insurance varies depending on your business, but it is generally available to protect your company's reputation from the fallout of data breaches, cyber-attacks, ransomware, automobile, trucking or workplace accidents, disruption in supply chain, negative press reviews, active shooters, kidnapping, extortion and hostage negotiation. You name it, there may be money available to help salvage your company's reputation because of these unforeseen and highly damaging fallouts.

Business Overhead Insurance. The last type of insurance you may want to consider if you are an entrepreneur is a business overhead insurance policy. Remember, the disability insurance mentioned above covers a percentage of your income but doesn't cover the payment of overhead expenses. Business Overhead policies typically cover the tax-deductible business expenses, such as office rent, salaries and benefits. This type of policy covers actual expenses, not lost profits, but is very helpful in instances where you have high overhead, so it may pay to look into this policy as well. Because you don't want to lose your business due to your incapacitation.

If you're overwhelmed on what insurance policy is right for your business, or you need some help navigating the different companies, consider using a broker. They earn their commission from the insurers, so this option comes at no cost to you but can save you a considerable amount of time and headache, and potentially your business. Don't wait until after the fact, because by that time, it's too late.

Even God Rested

"*Amid all your duties, keep some hours to yourself.*"

— Margaret Fuller

BY THIS POINT in your entrepreneurial endeavor, you are probably burning the candle at both ends, rarely relaxing and taking time out to rejuvenate yourself. I have one word for you: *relax*. I realize that this sounds counterintuitive, but that is exactly what you need to do. You've heard the saying, "Too much of a good thing is never a good thing." That applies even with your entrepreneurial endeavor, and I speak from experience.

Resting is different than saying "no." Saying no is about setting necessary boundaries to achieve your success and peace of mind. Resting is physical and mental rejuvenation. You can't rest if you are continuously saying "yes" to something. Get the difference?

My last semester in law school, I began divorce proceedings, in what could not have been worse timing. As we touched on in an earlier Tea Time, I decided to move back to Los Angeles from New York and take the California Bar Exam. Everyone, from my law school counselors to my parents, were horrified at my timing. It's very difficult to take and pass the California bar, which is known to be the most difficult in the country. California's exam was a three-day bar, when all other states at the time were two-day bar exams, and it statistically has the lowest pass rate of all state bars in the country. On top of the stress of getting divorced, and moving across the country, I attended New York University, whose courses were geared towards common law and some New York specific courses…and I hadn't taken any classes in California-specific law. So, the odds were doubly stacked against me.

When I arrived at the bar preparation class in Los Angeles, the instructor looked at the group and said: "I know you are all worried about passing the bar, and that is certainly understandable. This is a tried-and-true method here, so if you follow our guidance and keep up with the class work and assignments, you *will* pass the bar, and pass it on the first try." *Hmph!* I remember thinking. That was a *huge* proclamation, considering the low pass rate of the California Bar and my current situation! But he believed, and so did I, so I was going for the gold!

Their method was, they gave us the tools: class and the study guides. But the secret sauce was their schedule: a 6/1 formula — follow the class and study the plan for six days, and take one day off. This was two decades before anyone ever heard of self-care. The one day was dedicated to us to rest, where we didn't *think* about the bar, our classes, or studying. I am advising you to do the same thing: take a day off. They told us to go to lunch, spend time at the beach, go to the movies, catch up with our families—do whatever nourished our spirits at the time, and that is what I did. Their rationale is that it was a marathon not a sprint, and you will burn yourself out if you are singularly focused on anything.

But preparation here is the key, just as we've discussed in this book. I am giving you a formula, just as our instructors gave us the formula, and I stuck to it. I attended classes every morning, took a 90-minute lunch break, then hit the books again from 2:00 to 8:00. I basically studied for 10 hours a day, but I took time out, went to lunch, and <u>relaxed</u> during that time. I also found a beautiful, scenic place to study—Pepperdine University's law library, which overlooks the Pacific Ocean—with like-minded people who formed a study group. One friend, Bainy, saw me from across the lecture hall during the first week of studying and told me that I looked seriously prepared and she wanted to study with me. "Sure," I said, "but I have my program and this is my schedule. If you want to join, let's do this." And we did. We studied hard, we pushed each other, tutored each other in areas where one of us was stronger than the other, gave each other moral support, and we took the same days off. And we both passed on the first try. We never pulled an all-nighter, and never fell behind. We followed a plan of preparedness and had time to rest and reset our bodies and minds.

Just as you need to stick to a plan in order to succeed, you also need rest and rejuvenation. Feed and water your dreams, but don't drown them. Working around the clock is not sustainable; just ask anyone who's tried. The goal is to work smarter, not harder. So, whether your partner picks up the slack on that day, or whether you just shut it down for a day and binge watch movies and rejuvenate your soul, it is imperative that you take some time to rejuvenate so you can successfully complete this marathon!

Over the last few years, the term "self-care" has become part of our lexicon. There is a reason for that. Americans work longer hours than people in any other country. In Europe, by contrast, many cafés and shops are closed for a few hours in the afternoon between lunch and dinner. In fact, in France, resting and closing in between meals is the norm. So, some French restaurants *advertise* that they stay open, offering uninterrupted service with the words *Service Continu* (which literally means Continuous Service) plastered in their windows, because that continuous service is the exception, not the rule. In France, they have a 38-hour work week and it is illegal for an employer to contact an employee outside of work hours. A European employee has at least six weeks of vacation. In August, many of the boutiques and shops are closed so the proprietors can spend time with their families, and as a result, many of the cities in Europe are like ghost towns during that last month of summer. To mark the end of the summer shutdown in France, the first week in September is called *La Rentrée* ("The Return"), marking return from vacation life to city life, and life returning to normal. You get my point. Americans are the ones working ourselves to death, literally. Don't be one of them.

And if that isn't enough, just take a lesson from the Good Book, the Bible: Genesis 2:2-3: "By the seventh day, God had finished the work (S)He had been doing, so on that day, (S)He rested from all of Her Work. God blessed the seventh day and made it holy. (S)He blessed it from all the work (S)He had done." Even in the Bible, God rested on the Seventh Day.

If the Lord rested, you better believe you should too!

APPENDICES

A. Mutual Non-Disclosure Agreement

B. Trademark Class Appendix

C. Work for Hire Agreement

APPENDIX A

MUTUAL NON-DISCLOSURE AGREEMENT

This Financial Non-Disclosure Agreement (the "**Agreement**") is entered into as of _____, 2022 (the "**Effective Date**"), by and between _____ ("Company") on the one hand, and _____("_____") on the other (collectively, the "Parties" and each a "Party").

WHEREAS, the Parties each have certain confidential information relating to their businesses which they desire to disclose to each other for the purpose of facilitating _____ ("Transaction") and each Party is willing to accept the other's information confidentially subject to the terms of this Agreement.

NOW THEREFORE, in consideration of the mutual covenants and agreements contained herein and for other good and valuable consideration, the receipt and sufficiency of which is hereby acknowledged, the Parties agree as follows:

1. "**Confidential Information**" means any information furnished or disclosed, in whatever form or medium, by one Party (the "**Discloser**") to the other Party (the "**Recipient**") relating to the business of the Discloser, and includes, without limitation, financial institution records, tax records, sales revenues, forecasts, accounting records, investment holdings, wages or income information, or any other financial information that, if disclosed, could affect the Transaction. Confidential information also includes related information that may be disclosed in connection with

financial information, including but not limited to identification and account numbers, PINs, passwords, the identity or financial status of investors or partners, contract terms, financial information, business procedures, processes, techniques, methods, ideas, discoveries, inventions, processes, developments, records, product designs, clients, client information, work product, product planning and trade secrets, all of which is deemed confidential and proprietary.

2. The Recipient agrees to keep confidential all of Discloser's Confidential Information and to take all reasonable steps to preserve the confidential and proprietary nature of such Confidential Information. The Recipient also agrees to use Discloser's Confidential Information only for the purposes of the proposed Transaction, and will make no use of Discloser's Confidential Information, in whole or in part, for any other purposes. The Recipient agrees to refrain from disclosing Discloser's Confidential Information to third parties, except to its attorneys, business advisors and accountants, who agree to keep such information as Confidential, unless the Discloser has given its prior written authorization.

3. Notwithstanding any other provisions of this Agreement, each Party acknowledges that Confidential Information will not include any information that the Recipient can demonstrate: (a) was publicly available at the time of disclosure, or later became publicly available through no act or omission of the Recipient; (b) was already in its rightful possession at the time of disclosure; (c) was rightfully received by the Recipient from a third party without any obligation of confidentiality; or (d) was independently developed by or for the Recipient without use of Discloser's Confidential Information.

4. In the event that the Recipient is requested or required by subpoena or other court order to disclose any of

Discloser's Confidential Information, the Recipient will provide immediate notice of such request to the Discloser and will use reasonable efforts to contact the other Party and cooperate with the other Party so that an appropriate protective order may be sought, or a waiver of compliance with the provisions of this Agreement granted. If, in the absence of a protective order or the receipt of a waiver hereunder, the Recipient is nonetheless, in the written opinion of its counsel, legally required to disclose Discloser's Confidential Information, then, in such event, the Recipient may disclose such information without liability hereunder, provided that the Discloser has been given a reasonable opportunity to review the text of such disclosure before it is made and that the disclosure is limited to only the Confidential Information specifically required to be disclosed.

5. The Discloser may elect at any time to terminate further access to its Confidential Information. Upon written request, the Recipient will return to the Discloser all Confidential Information in any form and promptly destroy any and all material or information derived from the Confidential Information.

6. This Agreement and the obligations of confidentiality and nondisclosure contained herein will remain in full force and effect for the period of the term of the transactions discussed herein Agreement plus two (2) years ("Term").

7. The Confidential Information protected by this Agreement is of a special character, such that money damages would not be sufficient to avoid or compensate for any unauthorized use or disclosure of the Confidential Information. The Parties agree that injunctive and other equitable relief would be appropriate to prevent any such actual or threatened unauthorized use or disclosure. The remedy stated above may be pursued in addition to any other remedies available at law or in equity, and the Recipient agrees to

waive any requirement for the securing or posting of any bond in connection with such remedy. In the event of litigation to enforce any provision hereof, the prevailing Party will be entitled to recover all costs, including its reasonable attorneys' fees and costs, incurred in connection with the litigation.

8. Each Party agrees that during the Term and for a period of one year thereafter, a Party shall not at any time induce or attempt to induce, directly or indirectly, for itself, or on behalf of their company, any person, firm, company, corporation or entity, any of the employees or independent contractors of the other Party to leave the employ or discontinue working for or representing the Disclosing Party.

9. The Discloser warrants and represents that, to the best of their knowledge, the Confidential Information is truthful and accurate and may be used in reliance and evaluation of the Transaction hereunder.

10. This Agreement will be governed by the laws of California, without reference to rules regarding conflicts of law. Each of the parties hereto irrevocably consents to the exclusive jurisdiction and venue of the federal and state courts of the Los Angeles County, California.

11. No waiver of any term, provision or condition of this Agreement, whether by conduct or otherwise, in any one or more instances, will be deemed to be or be construed as a further or continuing waiver of any such term, provision or condition or as a waiver of any other term, provision or condition of this Agreement.

12. If any provision of this Agreement is determined by any court of competent jurisdiction to be invalid or unenforceable, such provision shall be interpreted to the maximum extent to which it is valid and enforceable, all as determined by such court in such action, and the remaining provisions of this Agreement will, nevertheless, continue

in full force and effect without being impaired or invalidated in any way.

13. This Agreement constitutes the Parties' entire Agreement with respect to the subject matter hereof and supersedes any and all prior statements or agreements, both written and oral. This Agreement may not be amended except by a writing signed by the Parties.

14. This Agreement shall be effective on the Recipients' employees, officers, directors and assigns.

15. By signing below, the Party states that each has carefully read this Agreement, and has been given a sufficient opportunity to consult counsel of that Party's choice with respect to entering into this Agreement, or has deliberately refrained from doing so, and that that Party fully understands this Agreement's full and binding effect and is signing this Agreement voluntarily.

IN WITNESS WHEREOF the Parties have caused this Agreement to be executed by their duly authorized representatives as of the date first referenced above.

(INSERT COMPANY NAME) (INSERT COMPANY NAME)

By:_____   **By:**_____

Its:_____   **Its:** _____

APPENDIX B:

Trademark Classes (as of January 2022)		
Class	**Type**	**Description of Goods**
Class 1	Chemicals	Industry, science and photography, agriculture, horticulture and forestry; unprocessed artificial resins, unprocessed plastics; adhesives for use in industry; putties and other paste fillers; compost, manures, fertilizers; biological preparations for use in industry and science, fire extinguishing and fire prevention compositions; tempering and soldering preparations; substances for tanning animal skins and hides.
Class 2	Paints and varnishes	Paints, varnishes, lacquers; mordants; raw natural resins; metals in foil and powder form for painters, clothing dye, colorants for food and beverages.
Class 3	Cosmetics and Cleaning Preparations	Cleaning, polishing wax, deodorants, scouring and abrasive preparations (sandpaper); soaps; perfumery, essential oils, cosmetics, hair

		lotions; dentifrices; Bleach and other substances for laundry use.
Class 4	Fuels and Lubricants	Lubricants, dust absorbing; industrial oils and greases; fuels (including motor spirit); candles and wicks for lighting, wetting and binding compositions.
Class 5	Pharmaceuticals	Pharmaceutical and veterinary preparations; dietetic food adapted for medical use or baby food; plasters, materials for dressings; material for stopping teeth, dental wax; disinfectants; preparations for destroying vermin; herbicides and fungicides.
Class 6	Metal and Alloy	Common metals and their alloys; metal for building and construction; non-electric cables and wires of common metal; ironmongery, small items of metal hardware; safes, metal containers for transportation and storage.
Class 7	Machinery and Tools	Machines, power operated tools and machine tools; agricultural implements other than hand-operated; incubators for eggs, automatic vending machines, motors and engines (excluding land vehicles).
Class 8	Hand Tools	Hand operated hand tools and implement (including drills, cutting tools); razors; cutlery; side arms (excluding fire arms).

Class 9	Scientific and Research Apparatus	Scientific and research and lifesaving equipment, photographic, cinematographic, optical, weighing, measuring, signaling, checking (supervision), equipment for recording, transmission or reproduction of sound or images; apparatus for controlling air and water vehicles (GPS) recording discs; automatic vending machines and mechanisms for coin-operated apparatus; cash registers, calculating machines, data processing equipment and computers; life-saving and teaching equipment and instruments; apparatus and instruments for conducting, switching, transforming, and controlling electricity; diving suits, nose and ear plugs for divers, masks, SCUBA equipment, fire extinguishers .
Class 10	Medical and Surgical Equipment	Surgical, medical, dental and veterinary equipment and instruments, bandages, orthopedic articles; massage gear, suture materials, artificial limbs, surgical implants, artificial eyes and teeth.
Class 11	Environmental Control Apparatus	Apparatus for lighting, heating, steam generating, cooking, refrigerating, ventilating, drying, water supply and sanitary purposes. Ovens, air conditioners, fireplaces, thermal collectors.

Class 12	Vehicles	Vehicles, Apparatus for locomotion by land, air or water. Transmission for land vehicles, remote control vehicles (excluding toys)
Class 13	Firearms	Firearms (hunting and sporting); explosives; fireworks; ammunition and projectiles. Bandoliers for weapons, rocket flares.
Class 14	Jewelry and Precious Stones	Precious metals alloys and goods coated in precious metals, clocks and watch and their components.
Class 15	Musical Instruments	Musical instruments, stands for musical instruments, parts of musical instruments, including strings, pedals, reeds, music boxes.
Class 16	Paper and Printed Matter	Paper, cardboard and goods made from same which not included in other classes, instructional and teaching materials, paint brushes; typewriters and office machines (excluding furniture); instructional and teaching material; printers' type and printing blocks.
Class 17	Rubber Goods and Electrical Materials	Processed and unprocessed rubber, gutta-percha, gum, asbestos, mica and goods made from these materials, adhesive tape and other materials (excluding household or medical purposes) and not included in other classes;, stopping and packing insulating materials; flexible non-metal piping.

Class 18	Leather and Imitation Leather Goods	Leather and imitation leather, and goods made of these materials and not included in other classes; trunks and travelling bags; saddlery; umbrellas, parasols and walking sticks; animal hides and skins; whips, harness and saddlery.
Class 19	Nonmetal Construction and Building Materials	Construction and building materials (non-metallic); non-metallic rigid pipes for construction; building glass; stones (granite, marble, and gravel); asphalt, pitch and bitumen; non-metal monuments.
Class 20	Furniture and Articles	Non-metal furniture which are not included in other classes, including that made of plastic, wood, cork, ivory, reed, cane, wicker, shell, horn, bones, amber, mother-of-pearl, meerschaum and substitutes for all these materials,.
Class 21	Household Utensils and Glass	Household or kitchen utensils and containers (excluding forks, knives and spoons), including corkscrews, servers and ladles; brush-making materials, combs and sponges; brushes (except paint brushes); steel wool; articles for cleaning purposes; unworked or semi-worked glass (excluding glass used in construction); glassware, porcelain and terracotta not included in other

		classes (piggy banks, vases and bottles).
Class 22	Ropes, Strings, and Synthetic Materials	Yarns and string used for textile use. Sacks, padding and cushioning. Tents, awnings; raw and fibrous textile materials and materials used in connection therewith
Class 23	Yarns and Fibers for Textile Purposes	Natural and synthetic textiles and threads. Fiberglass, elastic and rubber used in textiles
Class 24	Fabrics and Textile Substitutes	Fabrics and covers for household use; bed and table covers; sleeping bags, heated blankets.
Class 25	Clothing	Clothing, headgear and footwear and parts thereof.
Class 26	Embroidery, Lace and Hair Adornments	Lace and embroidery, braids and ribbons, buttons, hooks and eyes, pins and needles; artificial flowers. Zippers, buckles. Wigs and toupees.
Class 27	Floor Coverings	Mats, matting, carpets, and rugs, linoleum and other materials for covering existing floors; Non-textile wall hangings.
Class 28	Toys, Games and Sporting Goods	Games, toys, and playthings; sporting articles and gymnastic not articles included in other

		classes; Christmas tree decorations. Video games
Class 29	Meat, Fish and Processed Foods	Fish, meat, poultry and game and their extracts; jams, jellies, compotes; preserved, frozen, dried and cooked fruits and vegetables; eggs, milk and milk products; fats and oils used in foods.
Class 30	Foodstuffs and Staple Foods	Coffee, artificial coffee, tea, cocoa, sugar, rice, pasta, tapioca, sago; flour and preparations made from cereals, bread, pastry and confectionery, spices, herbs and seasonings; yeast, baking-powder; treacle, honey; mustard, salt; vinegar, condiments; spices; ice.
Class 31	Unprocessed Agricultural Products	Agricultural, horticultural and forestry products in their raw and natural states; fresh fruits and vegetables; seeds, herbs, malt, natural plants and flowers; foodstuffs for animals; cereal.
Class 32	Beer and Non-alcoholic Beverages	Beers; fruit drinks and fruit juices; mineral and aerated water, other non-alcoholic drinks; syrups and other provisions for making beverages.
Class 33	Wine and Spirits	All alcoholic beverages, except beers. Wines, spirits, de-alcoholised beverages; bitters.

| Class 34 | Smokers' Items | Tobacco; cigars, cigarettes, vaporizers, and other smokers' items; matches. |

SERVICES

Class No.	Type	Description of Services
Class 35	Advertising and Business. Office Function Services	Advertising and promotional services; business administration and management, business; office functions.
Class 36	Banking and Financial Services	Insurance; financial; monetary affairs; real estate services. EFTs; credit and debit card processing, Appraisals.
Class 37	Construction and Repair Services; oil and gas drilling	Building construction and repair and rental services (including bulldozing, cranes); roofing, installation services. Oil and gas.
Class 38	Telecommunication Services	Telecommunication, including digital and electronic means. Radio and television broadcasting.
Class 39	Transportation and storage; Travel	Transport including by rail, air, water; packaging and storage of goods; travel arrangement. Ferries,

		bridges; parking. Rental of storage containers
Class 40	Recycling; Treatment of Materials; Printing Services	Treatment of materials, waste and trash recycling, air and water purification and treatment. Preservation of food and drink.
Class 41	Education; Entertainment, Training	Education; entertainment; sporting and cultural activities; training services. Arranging and conducting conferences; amusement and recreation services;
Class 42	Technology and Scientific Services; Research and Design	Computer hardware and software design and development; laboratory services; industrial research and design. Engineering and scientific estimates and evaluations.
Class 43	Restaurants and Hotels	Food and drink preparation and rentals; providing services for temporary lodging. Boarding services for animals.
Class 44	Medical, Veterinary, Beauty & Forestry	Medical services; alternative healing; veterinary services; hygienic and beauty care by enterprises or persons; agriculture, horticulture;

		aquaculture, and forestry services.
Class 45	Legal and Security Services	Legal services; security services for the protection of real and tangible property and persons; personal and social services by others to meet the needs of individuals; funeral, and matrimonial services.

APPENDIX C:

WORK FOR HIRE AGREEMENT

This Agreement dated _____, 2022 is by and between _____ ("Company") and _____ ("Contractor"). Reference is hereby made to that certain project entitled "_____" (the "Project") for which Contractor is performing services as a _____. The parties hereby agree as follows:

Contractor, for good and valuable consideration in the amount of _____ ($_____) receipt of which is hereby acknowledged, hereby certifies and agrees that (i) all of the results and proceeds of the services of every kind heretofore rendered by and hereafter to be rendered by Contractor in connection with the Project, including, without limitation, any performance and sounds recordings by Contractor and (ii) all ideas, suggestions, dialogue, plots, themes, stories, characterizations and any other material, whether in writing or not in writing, at any time heretofore or hereafter created or contributed by Contractor which in any way relate to the Project or to the material on which the Project will be based (collectively, "Material") are and shall be deemed works "made-for-hire" for Company. Contractor further acknowledges, certifies and agrees that as between Contractor, on the one hand, and Company, on the other hand, Company is and shall be deemed the sole author and/or exclusive owner of all of the Material for all purposes and the exclusive owner throughout the universe of all of the rights comprised in the copyright thereof, and of any and all other rights thereto (collectively, "Rights"), and that Company shall have the right to exploit any or all of the foregoing in any and all media, now known or hereafter devised, throughout the universe, in perpetuity, in all languages as Company determines. If under any applicable law the Material is not deemed or otherwise considered a work-made-for-hire for Company, then to the fullest extent allowable and for the full term of protection otherwise accorded to Contractor under such applicable law (including any and all renewals, extensions and revivals thereof), Contractor hereby irrevocably assigns and transfers to Company the Rights and, in connection therewith, any and all right, title and interest of Contractor in the Project and any other works now or hereafter created containing the Material. Contractor will, upon request, execute, acknowledge and deliver to Company such additional documents consistent herewith as Company may reasonably deem necessary to evidence and effectuate Company's rights hereunder, and hereby grants to Company the right as Composer's attorney-in-fact to execute, acknowledge, deliver and record any and all such documents if Contractor shall fail to execute same within five (5) days after receipt from Company. Contractor hereby grants Company the right to change, add to, take from, translate, reformat or reprocess the Material and the Project in any manner Company may in its sole discretion determine, and Contractor hereby waives any benefits of any so-called "droit moral" or "moral rights" or any similar law in any jurisdiction throughout the universe. Contractor warrants that, except as contained in material furnished to Contractor by Company, all literary, dramatic, musical and other material and all ideas, designs and inventions of Contractor in connection with the Project are or will be original with Contractor or in the public domain throughout the world, shall not infringe upon or violate any copyright of, or to the best of Contractor's knowledge, infringe upon or violate the right of privacy or any other right of any person and, to the best of Contractor's knowledge, are not the subject of any litigation or claim that might give rise to litigation, and that Contractor is free to grant all rights granted and make all agreements made by Contractor herein. Contractor agrees to hold Company and its successors, licensees and assigns harmless from and against all damages, losses, costs, and expenses (including reasonable outside attorneys' fees and costs) which Company or any of its successors, licensees or assigns may suffer or incur by reason of any uncured material breach of any of the warranties made in this paragraph.

In the event of any breach by Company of the Agreement, the sole remedy of Contractor shall be an action for money damages actually suffered by Contractor, if any, and Contractor shall not have any right to enjoin, restrict or otherwise interfere with Company's rights in the Material or enjoin or restrain the financing, development, Project, exhibition, distribution and/or other exploitation of the Project.

Contractor shall promptly execute and deliver to Company within five (5) business days after receipt thereof, any and all instruments or other documents consistent herewith that Company reasonably deems desirable or necessary to effect, secure, protect, maintain, evidence and/or enforce any provision of this Agreement, and Contractor hereby appoints Company as its attorney-in-fact to execute any such documents in Contractor's name and/or on Contractor's behalf and to institute and/or prosecute such proceedings as Company may, in its sole discretion, deem expedient to effect, secure, protect, maintain, evidence and/or enforce its rights hereunder in the event Contractor is unable or otherwise fail to do so as provided herein, which power is coupled with an interest and therefore irrevocable. Company shall provide Contractor with copies of all documents executed by Company pursuant to its authority under this paragraph, provided that no inadvertent failure to do shall be deemed a breach of this Agreement.

Company and Contractor are independent contractors with respect to each other, and nothing in this Agreement will create any association, partnership, joint venture or agency relationship between them. Contractor acknowledges that Company will not be providing Contractor or any of its employees, contractors, or agents with any manner of workers' compensation or any other type of insurance coverage, nor will Company be withholding from any amounts payable hereunder, any federal, state, local and foreign taxes, including but not limited to, any social security taxes, disability, or unemployment insurance payments, nor any duties, tariffs, levies and similar assessment taxes. Contractor agrees to be solely responsible for any and all such amounts, and agrees to fully indemnify and hereby hold Company harmless from and against all such amounts, as well as from and against any and all claims arising out of the disability or injury of any of Contractor's employees, contractors, or agents to the extent that such indemnity is enforceable at law.

This Agreement will be governed by and construed in accordance with the laws of the State of _____ applicable to contracts entered into and fully performed therein.

Company's rights in the Material and Rights may be assigned, licensed, or otherwise transferred, and this Certificate of Engagement shall inure to the benefit of Company's successors, licensees and assignees, however Contractor's rights under this Agreement may not be transferred. Any purported assignment shall be *void in abnitio.*

IN WITNESS WHEREOF, the parties hereto have executed this Agreement as of the Effective Date.

By: CONTRACTOR   **By: COMPANY**

_____   _____

Signature   Authorized Signature

ACKNOWLEDGMENTS

I never understood a passion project until I set out to write this book. This was truly a labor of love that sometimes sucked the life out of me, but with the help of so many people and their encouragement, I made it to the finish line.

Firstly, I want to thank God, my Source, the inspiration from whom my life and all blessings flow. I have seen Her show up in so many ways and places in my life and the lives of others, I know without a doubt that She is real and that I am a child of the Most High. My daily prayer is that people see me and know what is possible with God in their lives.

To my mother, Louisa Thompson, who at times was a divorcée, a single mother raising three kids. I know it wasn't easy but you sacrificed to give your children the best education and the best in life. You'd never knew that we weren't born with the proverbial silver spoon. Mommy, you epitomize the meaning of hard work and dedication to your family and your craft. You showed me what is means to be selfless, to be of service by giving my time, treasures and talents, how to be a leader, to be self-reliant (maybe too self-reliant), and how to be classy and fabulous.

To my dad, Erwin Handley. What a ride! We had quite a complicated relationship for so many years but we finally made peace with our differences. But your life lessons taught me well. Your hard work and dedication set the bar high, as did your wanderlust. I can say I got it honestly. You instilled in me an indelible work ethic, preaching I had to work twice as hard to get half as far. You taught me about "sticktoitiveness" and so many times when I wanted to quit writing this book, I drew on that lesson to get me across the finish line. I pray that you are smiling down and proud of me.

To my bonus dad, Jeter Thompson. I gave you hell in the beginning, but you won me over and you were the best of the best. My father in every way that mattered. Thank you for pouring into me, you were second to none.

To my ancestors: my maternal and paternal grandparents. I think about each of you every day. Because of you, I am.

My brothers, Bucky and Eric, I learned so much from each of you. Being your "little sister" taught me love, resilience, life lessons, hard work. (You see a family theme here). You were examples of what it is to be great. And because of you, I learned to speak up for myself, and never take anyone's sh*t.

My nephewsons: Eric Jr., my "first born," Grant, my lap baby, and Jason, the youngest who never listens. You each bring me so much joy. My life is fuller because of each of you.

Gus, Susan and Shannon, you are more my siblings than cousins. We are a small but mighty bunch, and the only ones I could be a big sister to. We had so much fun growing up, and to this day, our bond continues. Shannon, I pray you are looking down and approve of my hair and nails. May you rest well, cuz!

Aunt Theresa, nobody can burn in the kitchen like you. Thank you for the comfort of food and family over the years and being a second mom.

Tandra, you are family in every way possible, I don't remember a time when you were not in our lives. Thank you for so much love and laughter and for being the glue.

Carolyn, you are a true inspiration because you live life to the fullest. Your *joie de vivre* is infectious, it's impossible not to have fun around you!

To my very first BFFs, Melyney and San, my sisters from another mister. Our bonds remain so strong to this day, even across the miles y'all continue to hold me down. You are truly my family.

(Ernest) aka Lamont Greer: OMG, what a ride! So many good times from riding together to school in the Lou, to Boston,

Chicago and now ATL. You're always there for me in every way. We all need a ride-or-die like you!

Tracey Brown James, my first college girlfriend: Thank you for so many good times. How many times did I fall asleep in a club with my head against a speaker?! You gave me a second family; a home away from home that started at BC and continues to this day. And thank you for the incredible honor of being the god-mother to your beautiful children, Harmon and Caleb.

My Original Basketball Wives crew: Crystal McCrary McGuire, Tonya Lewis Lee and Rita Ewing: I have so much history with each of you, individually and collectively. From the Knicks to nearly 30 years later, we are unbreakable! Who could envision back in the day where we'd end up, still thick as thieves? Too many good times to mention, and I love each of you dearly. Each of you knew me before I was a lawyer and each has trusted me with your legal endeavors. Thank you for believing in me.

My L.A. fam: Daphne Wayans, my original L.A. family. You poured so much into me and shared your family and holidays with me. Nikkole Denson-Randolph, from our "novel" intro-duction, I'm so grateful that he knew we would become friends for life! He ain't never lied. Cindi Smith, my original L.A. party girl, my cancer sister and forever friend. Donyell McCullough, for your infectious personality and optimism and always being a plug. Dina LaPolt, you have always propelled me to be great, you are the true embodiment of a "bad ass."

To my *Vibe* Crew: Kenard Gibbs, we reconnected after you saw me speak on a panel and brought me in as outside general counsel for the *hottest*, most groundbreaking magazine at that time. We made history: from the *Vibe* TV show, to the Vibe Awards, to Vibe Books, to *Spin* magazine, your "seeing" me changed my career! For 10 whole years, wow. Thank you. Emil, your creative vision and your eye is unparalleled. You are definitely a renaissance man in every aspect of the word. If I listed every person that I worked with over my tenure there, I'd have about five more pages, so just know that I see you, I appreciate what y'all did for the culture, and we are forever bonded by the *Vibe* years.

My NYC crew: Juliette Jones (aka Jules), my sis and world traveler, you are truly selfless and a friend that everyone needs. Nobody does Paris like us. We have so much of the world left to see. Bevy Smith: thank you for so many good times, but more importantly for pouring into me your words of encouragement over the years. When I wanted to give up on this book, you pushed me forward. To my "little one" Iesha, thank you for your friendship and sisterhood. The FRAM: Woady, Kiwan, Moochie, GoGo Stephie, C.J., Angelique: from the family dinners to birthdays and everything in between, our shenanigans over the years are unmatched. What happened there, stays there! Erika Munro Kennerly, the style maven. You called my name at Art for Life when I first moved back to NYC, and the rest is history. Thank you for always making me feel like family, which makes working together even more special. CarolArcher, my silent hitta with a heart of gold. Felita and Ramona, the dynamic duo, literally two of my first *new* friends when I moved *back* to NYC, and we're still going. Caralene, I stand in awe of you every day. You put the "p" in pivot—keep killing the game, sis. Christine, thank you for always being my creative sounding board and my go to TM maven. And Monica, my world class assistant! For 10½ years, you have kept me on point and held me DOWN. I couldn't do it without you! Know THAT!

My ATLiens: Lynn Whitfield: I didn't know where to put you because we started in N.Y. nearly 20 years ago, moved it to L.A., and now you are literally my neighbor in ATL, but always my FFL. Thank you for always holding me down and lifting me up. Grace, well, your name says it all, and you have to be one of the funniest and most talented women I know. Keep shining, sis. Michelle Sanchez-Boyce, Nelson Boyce: when you moved here, you brought a piece of N.Y. with you. Thank you for making ATL feel like home. Blythe Robinson, from day one you introduced me to your city, helping me navigate these unfamiliar waters. The Thursday Morning Coffee Crew: Pi, Zenith, Che, Charisse, when Blythe set up the group, who knew we'd still be going strong two years later. Thank you for making Covid bearable and for the circle of sisterhood. Curtis, my first new new friend when I moved to ATL, My Derek Jae: When I call, you are there no matter what. Not only for me, but my family. You are more than my stylist, you are a true friend! LisaLisa, Angela, and Eboni, thank you all for the wonderful introduction to your city and for keeping my finger on the pulse.

Rev. Carmen thank you for keeping me lifted, learning, and inspired and for helping propel me towards my best self.

To my lawyer crew: Tabetha, Brandii, Dina, Jagkeem, Denise, and Nathan. Although we are in the same industry, there is never any competition between us. May we continue to lift each other up as we climb. Stephen Barnes, thank you for being my very first mentor! Proof that your time spent pouring into me was time well spent, because look at us now; a full circle moment.

To my editors: Karen Good Marable, you pushed me, poured into me, and believed in this manuscript, thank you for holding my hand 'til the end! Miles Marshall Lewis, I am honored that you believed in this book enough that a big time, best-selling author like you would edit this "little engine that could!" Thank you both for making this great.

And lastly, to my clients, friends and supporters, too many to name: Because of you, this little spunky Black girl from St. Louis is able to live the life of her dreams. But the craziest thing is that there are *so* many of my friends that overlap as clients, and for that, I can't even begin to put my gratitude into words! The fact that each of you has trusted me literally with not only your livelihood, but the welfare of your families, your companies, and your reputations mean the absolute world to me. My career and life are better for your believing and trusting in me!

To all who have purchased this book: thank you. Just know that it *is* possible, and it's possible to do it all with style and grace.

NAMASTE!

ABOUT THE AUTHOR

Lisa Bonner, a successful entrepreneur for over 20 years, is a veteran entertainment and intellectual property attorney who provides counsel for large media companies, film distribution companies, producers, writers and publishers for her firm's music, television and film clients. Ms. Bonner is a frequent legal contributor on various television programs and provides legal editorial coverage for various print and online news outlets. Lisa also hosts *The LegaliTEA* a popular podcast that is syndicated on Apple, Spotify, Google Play and other platforms. Lisa lectures extensively on entertainment and intellectual property matters for various associations and law schools including Harvard Law School, ASCAP, and The Grammy Foundation.

An avid traveler, Lisa has traveled to 84 countries and has served as a travel journalist for several publications, including *YahooTravel!*, *Ebony* and *Essence* magazines.

Lisa is a critically acclaimed television producer on several productions including *Little Ballers,* which debuted on Nickelodeon which was nominated for a 2016 NAACP Image Award, *Little Ballers Indiana* and *Foreman,* the authorized biography of George Foreman which debuted on Epix. She currently has several television productions in development with various media companies.

Lisa graduated with honors from the University of Missouri-Columbia School of Journalism and received and a J.D. from New York University School of Law. She is a "Silver Star" Soror of Alpha Kappa Alpha Sorority Incorporated, a member of the International Women's Forum and a volunteer with Meals on Wheels. Lisa is a Board Member Emeritus of Break the Cycle, serves on the Board of Directors and Vice Chair for the National Black Arts Festival, and immediate past board member for Silence the Shame and the Bronze Lens Film Festival.